The New Retirementality

The New Retirementality

PLANNING YOUR LIFE AND LIVING YOUR DREAMS . . . AT ANY AGE YOU WANT

FOURTH EDITION

Mitch Anthony

WILEY

Cover image: Summer Reading © iStockphoto/YinYang
Cover design: Wiley

Published by John Wiley & Sons, Inc., Hoboken, New Jersey.

The first and second editions of the book were published by Kaplan Publishing. The third edition of the book was published by John Wiley & Sons, Inc.

Published simultaneously in Canada.

Library of Congress Cataloging-in-Publication Data:

ISBN 9781118705124 (Hardcover)
ISBN 9781118705100 (ePDF)
ISBN 9781118705025 (ePub)

Printed in the United States of America

10 9 8 7 6 5 4 3 2 1

This book is dedicated to my mother,
Bettie Anthony Huntley,
who has never been afraid to
blaze her own trails and follow her dreams.
A generous portion of her spirit
guides my life as well.

Contents

Preface

The world continues to awaken to the realities of this strange institution we have created called *retirement.* Ideas that sounded novel when I first wrote them down 12 years ago now appear to be fairly common sentiment. My inspiration for this fourth edition has come from both the 60-plus rebels who have decided to live life on their own terms, as well as insights from those much younger.

For example, Ryan (age six) is quite possibly a writer in waiting. He is the son of my wife's horse trainer. Ryan has visited with me in my library, where we discuss life, writing, and other macro themes that prevail upon the mind of precocious kindergartners. Recently, his mother sent this note to me:

> One day I was explaining what "retirement" meant to my son Ryan. He looked at me in a very puzzled way after digesting the meaning of this strange concept and then said to me, "Mommy, when I get older I will never retire because I am going to love my job." After pondering the concept for a minute longer he continued, "And you will never retire either will you Mommy? Because you love your job too; right?" I just laughed and reassured him that "No, I will probably never retire either because I truly do love my job." I smiled and thought how lucky he was at the young age of six to already have so much figured out. If only we could have more people entering our workforce with the focus not on that magical date of retirement, but rather on enjoying their journey through life and making the most of each day. Blcss our sweet children for reminding us what is important in life. . . .

As I was finishing writing this revision, I received a note from Marta, a woman in her 20s who had read an earlier edition, asking me if it had been published in Polish. I told her, regrettably, that it had not yet been published in Polish. I am half Polish, so I naturally felt an affinity toward Marta and inquired as to her reason for asking. Here's what she had to say:

> My parents are 55 and 54. Dad is in Afghanistan and mom moved back to Poland last year. Dad is ending his seventh tour this December and is going to "retire"—with mom—in Poland. I would like them to read your book because I'm afraid they are going to end up in a nut house with four padded white walls! Thirty years is a long time to do NOTHING. If they do not want to actually WORK FOR THE MAN, I want them to do SOMETHING. I just do not know the way to approach.

Neither Ryan nor Marta needed anyone to explain the rationale for wanting to fully retire to them. They instinctively understood, in viewing the idea through the lens of the soul, that retirement—as it has been fashioned and formed over the last 100 years—comes woefully short of helping human beings optimize their time on this planet.

Money is a part of the retirement discussion but is not the primary component, despite the modern cultural inferences of the term "retirement planning." What needs to be planned for is much bigger than the accumulation and distribution of your means. Don't get me wrong: having the means to retire is important. But what we also must plan for—but often don't—is meaning. Age is irrelevant when we discuss meaning at the individual level. Read and explore this book with an open mind and an even wider heart and I am confident that you, too, will cross the bridge toward the most meaningful stage of life yet.

Acknowledgments

This book has an audience primarily because of the belief and encouragement provided by literary agent and publishing consultant Cynthia Zigmund.

Whatever degree of refinement the reader finds in this text is due to the ever watchful and always caring eye of my wife and first-line editor, Debbie.

For her incisive eye and diligent archeology, I wish to thank my researcher, Nadia Marquez, for a job well done.

I wish to acknowledge the many authors quoted in this book whose ideas may have seemed to find the bleeding edge instead of cutting edge because they were ahead of their time. Their ideas about retirement life and changes are the seeds that have the power to ultimately enrich many frustrated souls.

M.A.

CHAPTER 1

A Short History of Retirement

"When I want to understand what is happening today, I try to decide what will happen tomorrow; I look back; a page of history is worth a volume of logic."

—Oliver Wendell Holmes

The U.S. standard-gauge railroad track is four feet, eight and one-half inches wide. Why such an odd measure? Because that was the width in England and the United States when railroads were built by British expatriates.

Where did the English get that measure? The first rail lines were built by the same people who built the tramways that preceded railroads, and they built the trams with the same jigs and tools used for building wagons. The wagons were built to what is now the standard-gauge railroad track so their wheels would fit the ruts of England's ancient long-distance roads.

The ruts had been made by the war chariots brought to England by the occupying imperial Roman army. And the chariots were four feet, eight and one-half inches wide to accommodate the rear ends of two horses. You're not alone if you struggle with change.

Retirement as we know it today is a relic from a time and a world that have long since passed. In the context of our modern age, conventional ideas about retirement are not just inappropriate—they are counterproductive. The concept of retirement was a shortsighted political machination and social manipulation that is no longer relevant and is hopelessly out of touch with our times.

Retirement is an unnatural phase in the modern life course. It is an insertion invented between work and death for purposes lying outside of those seeking to live a purposeful life. It is instructive for all of us to learn about the genesis of this life phase that was invented by a past society for purposes that are no longer relevant to most of us.

Retirement, as we understand it today, did not exist in preindustrial America. In those days, older members of society weren't sent to the sidelines. They actually held a more prominent place as a resource for their insight, knowledge of skills and crafts, and lessons gained from experience. It was the industrialization era that accelerated the conditions that gave us the traditional version of retirement. Industrialization ushered in a profound redefinition of work. Mass production became the popular mode of work, and workers began to be viewed as parts in the system, subject to wear and replaceable.

With the advent of industrialization came a population shift from the country to the cities. This brought about a significant lifestyle adjustment as people went from self-sufficiency to dependency. Work became a means to an end—an income to live on—as opposed to a way of life. In his book *The Sociology of Retirement* (John Wiley & Sons, 1976), Robert C. Atchley made an insightful comparison between a craftsman and a worker. A craftsman controls the process and the product, which makes his work both satisfying and integral to his identity. An industrial worker is responsible for one small part of the process. Consequently, the work offers little reward. Atchley also noted that the words *job* and *occupation* soon began to replace the terms *craft* and *vocation* in the American laborer's lexicon. We can trace a cycle of degradation of the American work ethic to this point in history, which comes as no surprise because you would naturally expect people to become lethargic about work that offers us no emotional reward.

As other nations were embracing industrialization, the world became a competitive commercial environment. America was intent on proving itself to be a world leader, and progress was the mantra of the industrialists. As a result, these industrialists began looking for ways to sweep away anything that stood in the path of progress. For some of them a major obstacle to progress was anyone considered "mature" in age. Because of advances in safety and health care, people were living longer and the workforce was getting older. Mature workers were beginning to be viewed as a threat to progress. It was assumed that older people would not acclimate easily to changing procedures, and changes were needed for industry to become an efficient, well-oiled machine. The seeds of ageism were beginning to be sown. Those seeds of prejudice were watered over a century ago by a widely reported speech by Dr. William Osler, one of the nation's most prominent physicians, given in 1905 at Johns Hopkins University. Osler's thesis was that any man over 40 years old was virtually useless to society.[1]

"Take the sum of human achievement in action, in science, in art, in literature," Osler said. "Subtract the work of men above 40, and while we would miss great treasures, even priceless treasures, we would practically be where we are today." In short, Osler was postulating that any person over 40 was dispensable to the cause of progress. Osler went on to say that people over 60 were "entirely useless" and a drain on society because of their inelastic minds. Osler's articulation helped to embolden a growing intellectual trend and opportunistically served to answer the growing societal problem of unemployment. It seemed obvious, these intellectuals asserted, to replace the old with the new. All that was left was to come up with a way to get rid of the old. Mandatory retirement was one answer.

Another emerging force in this drama was the labor union, which was struggling to survive and fighting for the right to strike. Labor unions quickly embraced the idea of retirement because forcing out the older workers gave them the opportunity to deliver the jobs and job security they were promising their membership. Business leaders, labor leaders, and social engineers were all singing the retirement chorus. Older workers didn't have a chance—and soon wouldn't have a choice.

There was, however, one massive obstacle standing in the way of this strategy. What would these new retirees live on? In the late 1800s, Chancellor Otto von Bismarck had come up with a disability insurance program in the German Empire for all disabled workers 70 and older. This was instituted by von Bismarck, in part, to undermine demands for democracy and to reaffirm workers' commitment to the government. Around that same time, American Express created the first private pension in America in 1875.[2] In 1900 the Pattern Makers League of North America became the first union to offer pensions to its members. Up until that time, pensions were typically available to veterans and some civil servants such as policemen and firefighters (and, in some states, teachers).

It was not until 1910 that the pension movement gained steam. That year, the Taft administration started promoting pensions as a major piece of its platform on industrial efficiency. From 1910 to 1920, more than 200 new pension plans were formed. A change in the corporate tax law that made pension plans more tax advantageous resulted in the doubling of new plans in 1920. Overall, the penetration rate for pensions was quite slow, with only 15 percent of American workers covered by a plan by 1932. The watershed moment came in 1933, in the deepest, darkest depths of the Great Depression. Social conditions had reached an explosive point because of the 25 percent unemployment rate. Franklin D. Roosevelt and the New Dealers were in a precarious and potentially disastrous situation, with masses of angry young men demonstrating in the streets. Roosevelt had already seen where these situations could lead by the examples set in Germany and Italy. It was exactly these conditions that gave rise to both Hitler and Mussolini. The New Dealers' plan to get young people working again was to offer a public pension so the older men would retire.

Combine this reality with the fact that a movement was afoot with the elderly to demand pensions for those over 60. People wanted the federal government to get involved. At that time, 28 states had pension programs—which made little difference in the lives of the recipients because the programs were sparsely funded as a result of the Great Depression. Many corporate pensions were defaulting as well. As a result, 50 percent of the elderly were living in poverty.

The New Dealers needed to test their plan before implementing it on a national scale. Would the older workers like the idea? Senator Robert F. Wagner introduced a bill in 1934 that established a pension for retiring railroad workers. Wagner compelled 50,000 workers to consider retiring immediately. The bill passed. Wagner played a major role in 1935 in persuading FDR to introduce the Older Workers Pension Act, later called the Social Security Act, the statute that would forever change our views of work and retirement. However, Roosevelt had to settle two major issues that would echo through the generations. How would Social Security be paid for, and at what age would workers become eligible? This Social Security program would not work if it failed to provide instant benefits for those who were currently at the retirement age. Rather than taxing these people for their own retirement, the politicians came up with the idea of taxing those who were still working on behalf of retirees. Tax the younger generation to pay for the retiring generation. When the Social Security Act was implemented, the number of beneficiaries was small enough that no one would have to pay much for the plan.

Now the biggest question had to be answered: at what age can one receive Social Security? Precedents existed at the time in Germany, Great Britain, and France, with ages pegged to 60, 65, and 70. Citing a biblical reference to "threescore and ten years," Bismarck's original retirement marker was set at 70, allowing the workers enough time to pick out a gravestone if they should be lucky enough to live much longer. Eighteen years later, Germany lowered the age to 65—because very few people lived to 70 to collect the benefits—the average life expectancy at that time was just 46 years!

The retirement plans designed by Bismarck and others had obviously not been intended to give a worker any time for enjoyment—not with a life expectancy of 46 and a retirement age of 65. It helps to move to our modern age to understand Bismarck's original intent. The age of retirement was 19 years beyond the average life expectancy. In those days a person who was 65 was indeed old—much older than today's 65-year-old.

When FDR and the New Dealers settled on the age of 65 in 1935, the average life expectancy in America was 63 years. Bear in mind, however, that life expectancy statistics can be misleading because factors such as infant mortality are calculated into them. In fact, according to the Social Security Administration the average number of years lived in retirement today hasn't changed much since 1935, increasing only about five years during that period.[3] The obvious conclusion one could make is that retirement was never intended to remove people with strong productivity potential out of the workplace. Our view is skewed on this issue, however, as a result of the difference in the constitution of a 65-year-old today and that of a 65-year-old in 1935. Because the retirement markers were set later than the average life expectancy, many people didn't live long enough to collect Social Security benefits. FDR eventually moved to have the age of retirement set to age 62.

The benefits that a retiree did receive were just enough to support a meager lifestyle, providing bare sustenance. It was this generation of retirees that evoked the images of widows wearing full winter gear for lack of heat in decrepit one-room apartments in the winter and eating cat food to survive. It would take another 20 years before the social net and workplace invention known as retirement would become a part of the American way of life.

The retirement lifestyle got a major boost during World War II when workers' wages were frozen. Because wages were nonnegotiable, union leaders began bargaining for pensions where they didn't exist and for bigger employer contributions where they did exist. These contributions were tax deductible, and future pension obligations weren't reflected in a company's balance sheet. World War II conditions caused pension coverage to flourish across most industries. The timing could not have been better for the Social Security system, which was being roundly criticized for allowing retirees to live in poverty. Opportunistic politicians in the following decades began to push for broadened coverage to include husbands of working women, farmers, the self-employed, members of the armed forces, and so on. Coverage itself was expanded to include health and disability insurance, welfare for the disabled, and, as an answer to the senior poverty issue, annual cost-of-living adjustments to keep up with inflation.

With all these changes, retirement began to shed its destitute and forsaken image. Combining Social Security payments with pension checks allowed people to live out a respectable, if modest, retirement—but it still typically lasted only a year or two at best. It was during this period of retirement's image transition that financial services companies stepped up their efforts. They began to market retirement as *an individual's rightful reward for his or her years of labor and loyal service.* People began buying more retirement investment products and looked forward to an era of reward that would be timed on their new gold watch.

William Graebner, in his *History of Retirement* (Yale University Press, 1980), shares an interesting anecdote regarding a shift in the financial services industry's marketing of retirement. The story is told that in 1952, H. G. Kenagy of Mutual Life Insurance advised business leaders on the National Industrial Conference Board about the best way to sell retirement to their employees. The tack he suggested was distributing stories by these business leaders via company newsletters and the like about happily retired people fishing or playing golf and sipping martinis. Sell the blissful retirement life and don't forget to mention how to get to nirvana by investing in both the company plan and other financial vehicles. This was not a difficult story to sell to a workforce that now had jobs instead of vocations. As one 82-year-old nonretiree put it, "They that lack a vocation are always longing for a vacation." Retirement had now become the permanent vacation—without the kids! This retirement pitch from 1952 has hardly changed more than 60 years later. Although some firms in the retirement products industry are catching on to the philosophical shift regarding what people really want out of their longer lives, many companies in the industry lag woefully behind, with antiquated images of fishing ponds, beachside, and golf course heaven.

People began to retire in unprecedented numbers because (1) they felt they had to or were forced by retirement age policy to do so, and (2) the unexpected appreciation in home prices made comfortable retirement a real possibility. The implied message to workers: "You don't have a choice. Once you hit 62, you're out the door." No employers were begging them to stay around for a while or maybe to just cut back their hours. It was universally accepted that you were no longer welcome in the working world at retirement age.

Crossing the Bridge

We have, in years past, had our brains pummeled with warnings that we should save more if we hope to leap off the economic cliff known as "retirement" at age 62. Many of us had been convinced that we wanted to jump off that cliff earlier—if possible, much earlier. But, today, we understand that the new retirement resembles a bell curve rather than a cliff. Rather than jumping off a vocational cliff, we will gradually slow down.

The metaphor that I believe is more fitting for our age is that of a bridge between full-time work and full-time retirement. The length of the bridge varies from person to person, and the bridge can appear for any length of time and can be entered and exited multiple times in the post-60 years. And there are some of us who want to do the work we do as long as we possibly can—meaning as long as we are healthy and competent, we will be on that bridge.

A new realization around retirement has dawned as the result of the confluence of an asset-eroding economy and a cultural epiphany around retirement. The great recession convinced millions that a longer work life would be necessary, and many of those who had retired were returning to at least part-time work because they found something missing in the traditional vision of retirement.

The reality we are left with is that most of us will work longer than previously expected but not necessarily for reasons we assumed. Yes, economic incentives will play a role as many of us seek to replenish retirement funds or extend benefits, but the incentives don't begin and end with your checkbook—they are much more holistic than previously understood. Many of us are choosing to work longer for our own well-being, for the well-being of a relationship, and for the well-being of society.

Individual Retirement Attitude

One thing is for sure: We are no longer living with industrial-age realities, and the industrial machine should not be making life decisions on our behalf. As individuals, we need to decide when we are done. It should be a matter of personal policy, not corporate or government policy. The first order of business, then, is to eradicate artificially imposed finish lines in our life and begin designing our own track to run on.

CHAPTER 2

Removing Artificial Finish Lines

"Most people say when you get old you have to give things up, but I think we get old because we give things up."

—Theodore Green

(Senator Green was 98 when he retired in 1966.)

Whether you are 62, 65, or some other age at which you've been told you should retire, that number is nothing more than an *artificial finish line.* Only you have the right to announce a verdict on your date of extraction. The employment of your skills, competencies, and ideas should be for as long as you desire. None of us comes into this world with "use by" dates stamped on our backs. As long as we enjoy utilizing our competencies and truly love what we do, we should never quit the race. We may slow our pace or change the event we run in, but we should never stop participating.

Do you really want to quit working? Sadly, because so many people are working in jobs, industries, and offices they hate, they have convinced themselves that the answer is to stop working (aka, retirement). But the fact remains that most of us wouldn't be obsessed with the idea of quitting if we were doing what we wanted to do in the first place.

Many of us don't like the circumstances we find ourselves in—we feel stuck. We feel the only remedy is to quit working. This is akin to getting a frontal lobotomy because of a headache. Maybe the real truth is that you want to quit what you are currently doing to be able to do something else; you need or want a change but are convinced that you need a mountain of money to make the switch. You decide to postpone your dreams, assuming that when you finally do have the money, you will still have the desire and drive necessary to follow your dreams. People in these circumstances—and there are many—need to contemplate the psychologically sobering fact that as they drive themselves in a career they dislike (or worse, despise), they are driving on tires with a slow leak. The ride gets rougher and tougher until they find their aspirations in the ditch and little energy left to begin a new journey. This is what happens when you chase an artificial finish line.

Why have so many of us given our lives to work we don't enjoy? The reason is simply that we need the money. Why do we need the money? So we can have enough to retire at age 62 and finally do what we want. Great! You've just sacrificed 40 prime productive years in order to have a speculative, free rein for the autumn and/or winter years.

Doing work we despise or being in circumstances we deplore depletes our spirit. The reason many of us find ourselves in such scenarios is that we have been sold on an idea about retirement that is flawed to the core: *the idea that we should do what we do not enjoy to accumulate the money we need to someday do what we want.* This hope of doing what we really want to do is why the concept of traditional retirement is alluring to so many. Too many of us are not on the track we want to run on. We see getting to the age of 62 with enough money as the only way to get there. When you're on the wrong track, any finish line will do.

> *Once we become adults, we often lose track of life's simple pleasures and of our own personal goals. We take a wrong turn or two, then spend a good part of our lives doing things we'd rather not—while not doing many things we'd enjoy. While we may obsess about how unhappy we are, we don't focus clearly on what we can do to change the situation: on how we can invest our time, energy and, yes, our money to consciously create the life we want.*
>
> —Marc Eisenson, author,
> *Invest in Yourself: Six Secrets to a Rich Life*

There are two types of people who need to reexamine their plans for complete retirement at age 62 or 65—those who *can't* afford to retire and those who *can* afford to retire. It's worth repeating: age 62 is an artificial finish line. In the preceding generation the predominant measure of success was how many years you could retire ahead of age 62. Nobody thought that they were accelerating their pace into boredom and aimlessness because retirement was the career worker's badge of success. On the flip side, a measure of failure had been to measure how many years *beyond* 62 you had to wait so you could retire. The further past 62 you had to wait to retire, the greater failure you were in the context of retirement. Fortunately, all those measures are about to change.

If the coming generation of 60+-year-old citizens has anything to say about it, those perceptions will be turned entirely on their head. Those who have to work will not be the losers, because they are still in the game—they will find that work keeps them vital, involved, and healthier. Those who will be able to drop out entirely will choose not to because they don't want to enter a slow track of intellectual atrophy, boredom, and monotonous leisure.

Is accelerating your pace into boredom, "every day's a Saturday" all-play agenda really such a good idea? Unlike the nursery rhyme we learned as children, it's really "all play and no work" that makes Jack a dull boy. The illusion has been that of sipping tropical drinks on a Caribbean beach and setting tee times for the rest of your waking life. "All this is yours" once you retire, and the earlier you retire, the better. Possibly you've met some people who swallowed this illusion and are living with the hangover of boredom and purposelessness in their lives.

I have met many such people, and the look in their eyes inspired me to write this book. Many who bought the story of retiring from the race find themselves bored with not being in the race. Many have found that this boredom has led to self-destructive patterns of behavior. Many have accelerated their aging process as the chains of disenfranchised habits have grown heavier and weighed on their health. It all adds up to one inescapable conclusion: *Retirement is an unnatural condition! Even if you can afford to retire, the worst thing you can do is withdraw completely from the track of relevance!*

Although you may not have heard much about it, those who do get to the magic age of 62 and drop out of the race are not always altogether happy with their decision. Many have told me that they took retirement because they felt as though they had to. Disillusionment rates are sky high for retirees. According to a survey conducted by AARP and the Society for Human Resource Management, 20 percent of U.S. companies have programs in place to phase in retirement to avoid just such disillusionment.[1] There is a good reason these retirees are not happy—*retirement is an unnatural idea.* The concept runs contrary to the preservation of the human spirit. We will explore this idea in depth throughout this book.

Motivated by Autonomy

Most people don't really want retirement in the form we've observed during the past few generations. What we want is freedom to pursue our own goals and interests. We want autonomy to call our own shots. We want to do what we want, when we want, and where we want. We want change if our employment has become a dispiriting rut. We have been told that the right amount of money alone can buy that emancipation. And, if we believed that message, we may have settled into that rut and postdated our satisfaction for a time in the distant future. Our artificial finish line beckoned to us.

And that is why we are so vulnerable to the messages that tell us we need $2 to $3 million to set ourselves free. But this simply is not true. I will not argue that having money gives you options—it does. If you have enough, you can usually do things the way you want. But financial abundance is not the exclusive seed bed for autonomy. Willfulness with resourcefulness is the more potent soil for finding a work life that satisfies.

This book tells stories of people who are living the life they want—*today*—and not all have a million dollars in assets or investments. Because of outdated ideas around retirement, we have put the money cart ahead of the "life" horse. We say we are saving money so that we can someday have a life, but in the process we delay having a life so that we can scrounge up enough money. Too many people wait far too long to realize that the life we are living right now is not a dress rehearsal.

With some financial creativity and a new mind-set regarding retirement, you can both find *and* fund the life you really want—if not now, it is entirely possible within the next five years. Achieving emancipation in your working life will involve negotiating your lifestyle, philosophy, and fiscal habits, and finding a way to put first things first. First, decide the path you must take to do the work you love, and, second, put together a plan to pay for that privilege. All of us must adopt a much more resourceful approach if we hope to make the transition into a life of doing what we love. It won't necessarily be easy, but it will be worth it.

We are still in the early stages of a New Retirementality—a modern perspective of what retirement really means. People are still haunted by the old rules and media hype that bemoan their lack of preparedness to reach the artificial goal line. We just can't seem to get away from the news stories, retirement studies, and advertisements that beat this sorry old retirement message to death.

There is no doubt that as a society, we could exercise more discipline in our savings habits. Indeed, it wouldn't really harm us in the present to put more assets away toward our future. However, putting money away toward your future and putting money away toward your extraction from the work engagement are two different matters.

This point became especially clear to me recently when a friend asked me if I had plans to retire early. I thought about it for a moment, and then it dawned on me—*I like what I do!* I write, speak, and consult with companies on how to build more meaningful relationships. Why would I quit doing that? If I did quit, I think I would begin to feel aimless and lost. This realization was important because it helped me to realize that I no longer had to be concerned with having any specific amount of money at any specific age. There will always be something for me to do, and I will always enjoy doing it. You don't make plans to retire from your passion in life.

Does this idea cause me to spend away my future and disregard the value of my investment savings? To the contrary! *Because I value freedom so much, I exercise more than necessary financial discipline to maintain that freedom.* The idea of autonomy compels me, motivating me to exercise financial discipline in what I spend and what I save. I love my life, and I'm not going to put it at risk because I didn't have the prudence to put away a ransom toward my own freedom.

I know that I am just one foolish purchase or investment away from reattaching the chains of miserable employment to my life. There is wisdom in balance. The fact that I love what I do does not negate the need to plan for financial freedom. Life can present us with vicissitudes that can radically alter our course: disability, a death in the family, divorce, and so on. We must plan ahead financially because we change our minds over time. What invigorates me today may bore me a decade from today. Investment savings are necessary to purchase the freedom to change course when we want.

I find this idea much more compelling than saving toward a date where I will magically find myself, my dreams, and the freedom to do what I've waited 30-plus years to do. Yet I find it troubling, because of the constant media barrage and the financial services–induced discouragement, how many people are concerned about their inability to "retire" at 62 or 65. Pleeeease! Can we have a break from this man-made definition of success and take a closer look at reality?

An insightful financial advisor told me the following:

> If you were to ask me, "Who are the most distraught clients you see?" I think my answer would surprise you. They are not the ones who are discouraged to find out they will not be able to retire when they thought. They are not the clients whose portfolios have had less-than-spectacular returns and must extend their plans for early retirement. They are the retirees with the great portfolios who are bored out of their minds. These individuals feel like they have been removed from the mainstream of life, are watching from the sidelines, and are not allowed to get back in. As one guy put it, "Retirement is a spectator sport. I don't want to sit here and watch the world go by. I liked being in the game!"

Yet, strangely enough, millions are in a mad rush to get to the place where this despondent man lives—on the sidelines. Many of us, however, have already seen enough of our parents' and forerunners' retirement scenarios to know that this is not the life for us. We have figured out that our lives will be full of challenge, relevance, stimulation, and occupational adventure. We may slow down but we are not leaving the track for the concession stand.

The fortunate people who have the money are better able to understand what the money is all about—liberty to do what they want when they want. What is the point of using that kind of liberty to do nothing but play golf? It's hard to convince someone who doesn't have the money that it really is not about the money. It's about doing what you love, doing what you want. It's about balancing vocation and vacation. It's about balancing enrichment and relationships.

Illusions, Delusions, and Hype

Yet the drumbeat of "you won't have enough to retire" pounds on like a Sousa march without regard to the cultural realizations we are experiencing around the retirement experience of our parents and forerunners into the gated community existence. We will be hearing these messages for the foreseeable future until some marketing executives wake up and realize that making people feel worse about what they don't have isn't a great ploy for motivating the masses.

For many, these messages about retirement shortfalls or retirement readiness (by age 62) inspire urgency and thrift. For many others, they inspire only fear, self-loathing, and hopelessness. Such messages as "You won't have enough" or "If you had bought this fund 30 years ago, it would be worth *x* million dollars today" create a sense of dread and failure in those who were buying more dime bags than mutual funds with their disposable income 30 years ago.

In a 2012 survey by the Employee Benefit Research Institute, 60 percent of workers had less than $25,000 saved (excluding the value of their home).[2] For the millions of Americans who don't own a fat nest egg, these messages stir feelings of hopelessness because they are convinced that they will arrive at the age 62 economic leap with no safety net or precious metals parachute based on their current income and level of savings. They know they will never be able to amass the small fortune that "retirement experts" tell them they must hoard to have anything but a beggar's sunset in their life. The modern retirement portrait, as painted by the financial services industry, is truly a double-headed dragon, because the vision that has been promoted for the last 50 years is not only an illusion but is also unrealistic.

When you ask many retirees how they're doing, they often reply, "I'm keeping busy." This is an acknowledgment of the activity void that retirement has brought. Most humans are truly happy when they are busy doing what they love. If they are not busy, they are most likely not very happy.

The image of retirement that we have been sold has simply been untrue. According to an American Demographics poll, 41 percent of retirees report that retirement was a difficult adjustment. Only 12 percent of newlyweds polled felt that marriage was a difficult adjustment, and only 23 percent felt that parenting was a difficult adjustment. The reason the adjustment to retirement is difficult to so many is simple: Retirement as it has been defined for us was never meant to be. Retirement is an illusion because those who can afford the illusion are disillusioned by it, and those who cannot afford the illusion are haunted by it.

Which brings us to the dragon's other head: Many of us cannot afford to retire in the manner that has been promoted by the retirement savings industry. It is simply unrealistic for us to find a way to put away enough money every month to have millions waiting to serve us at age 62, or at any other age for that matter. But why should a significant percentage of our population that is doing its best with what it has walk around feeling discouraged about today because it cannot reach a tomorrow that somebody else has defined for it? We have been given the various ominous headlines for our future: "Social Security will not exist; your homes are devalued; you don't have sufficient savings, and inflation will eat up what little you do have." According to the Insured Retirement Institute, the majority of us expect to retire past age 66; while the reasons may be financial, intellectually we're better off.[3]

The most profound problem I see with pervasive and frequently reported scare tactics is that these arguments are founded on a fabricated and now crumbling philosophical foundation—that is, we *should* retire at age 62 or 65. Many of us will not completely retire at 65, and many will not retire at all. And one of the chief drivers of this trend will not be that we simply cannot afford to retire, it will be because we, as a generation, are not interested in artificial finish lines.

Individual Retirement Attitude

- The realization that retirement is an unnatural idea and runs contrary to the preservation of the human spirit.
- The freedom to stay in the race as long as you choose to.
- Prizing personal autonomy above all else.
- Being motivated to save and invest toward that personal autonomy.

The New IRA—Individual Retirement Attitude

"I used to get upset when a star player of our local team would take a big contract and head elsewhere to play. 'No team loyalty anymore,' I thought. After I was ceremoniously dismissed from my company after three decades' I realized why they do it. There's no team loyalty on the other side of the equation either. If you assume someone else has your best interests at heart, you assume wrongly."

—A sports fan

All one has to do to get in touch with modern economic realities of retirement is to take a look at the trend of the past decade away from the paternalistic pension approach toward the autonomy of defined contribution (DC) plans including 401(k) or 403(b). Pensions—also known as defined benefit (DB) plans—were originally designed to provide guaranteed benefits for the rest of your life, and in some cases, for the rest of your spouse's life. The percentage of people being covered by pension plans has been shrinking since 2000, and as of this writing (2013) 84 percent of employees in the public sector had pension plans, while only 21 percent in the private sector had them. But the migration from pensions to self-directed plans has already begun in the public sector and will be a massive trend going forward as more and more states and municipalities struggle to meet their pension liabilities.

The chief difference between a defined benefit and a defined contribution plan is who is on the hook of responsibility. Organizations have and are sending a clear message that they are not interested in being on that hook any longer. For decades, workers were like passengers on the retirement bus, leaving the driving and benefits planning to organizations. Today, however, we are being put behind the wheel of our own retirement savings vehicle and told to drive. What happens on the road ahead is entirely up to us.

Many DC plans originally came about because companies were failing and couldn't meet their pension obligations, but today's companies are doing away with pension programs for other reasons, most of which are related to sustainability. These days, even financially stable firms are doing away with pension plans. Employers like DC plans because they are cheaper to maintain, while employees like them because they are portable. In the days when pensions proliferated, people were afraid to walk away from careers they found unsatisfying for fear of losing the pension benefits that could sustain them for many decades. Today, without such pensions in place, most people can simply transfer their DC accounts into an individual retirement account (IRA) and portage their career efforts to other streams.

There has never been a more serious need for people to take responsibility for themselves and their own retirements. Many of the pensions that still exist are seriously underfunded. According to the Pew Center for the States, the underfunding is approximately $1 trillion. This massive amount is nothing more than hidden debt, representing an obligation owed where the promising party no longer has the resources to meet its obligations. For years I have written that the proper definition of a pension is *"a promise that is good until it's not."*

A closer look at the obligations assumed by the Pension Benefit Guaranty Corporation (PBGC) should give us all pause. The PBGC assumed the pension obligations of a number of failed airlines' pensions as well as those of steel companies and auto manufacturers. As of this writing (2013), the PBGC is underfunded by over $35 billion. Keep in mind the statistic in the previous paragraph ($1 trillion). Something clearly isn't adding up. Also bear in mind that the PGBC is the party *guaranteeing* the benefits of failed institutions.

More corporate pensions will fail in the next decade, as will many of those of states and large cities.

> *"The pension world is following a more Anglo-Saxon approach. More individualism, take care of yourself, not your neighbor."*
>
> —European employer

The reasons the private sector has largely done away with pension plans are manifold but include the fact that companies disliked having to report their actuarial soundness to the Department of Labor (there were penal fees for not reporting). This lack of reporting—as well as turning a blind eye toward critical information such as long-term perspectives on plan funding—is a critical factor in contributing to the underfunding of pension plans. Additional accounting hanky-panky comes into play when corporations often state pension benefits as assets, and use those assets to balance their budgets in order to stay in business. As absurd as it sounds, accounting rules allow firms to list those benefits as assets even when the firm is severely underfunded toward meeting those obligations.

On the public pension side of the matter, there are political drivers to blame for long-term insolvency in many of these public pensions. DB plans are funded by means of cyclical resources, meaning you would expect additional funding when times are good and possible cutbacks in funding when resources are scarce, but elected officials tend to cut pension funding when the markets are good and cut back on pension funding when markets are bad to balance budgets. Only politicians could come up with such an ingenious plan for hastening insolvency!

The developing scenario around public pension obligations will emerge as major concern for taxpayers in the coming years. Half of the state budget deficits of $11.4 billion projected for 2011 were due to pension-related expenses. Many state and local governments are following the acts of failing pension plans—like those of the airline industry—where market values of pension fund assets and liabilities are off the balance sheet (Statement of Net Assets) of state and local governments, which only delays the inevitable. Pensions are like bonds in that they are obligations to pay. When the entity cannot pay, they raise taxes or cut back on programs that currently benefit their employees.

My goal is not to paint a bleak portrait of the future but to prepare you for what lies ahead. The irreversible conclusion is that the onus is now squarely upon each and every one of us to assume responsibility for every aspect of our economic well-being. Some people make the argument that much of the European debt crisis can be traced to institutional obligations that were never realistic. Europeans who planned on retiring with full benefits at 58 years of age are now busy making other plans. My point is this: no one can afford to sit around expecting an institution to follow through on promises they have made, corporations and governments included. Some of the reality checks of this modern age are as follows:

- If you have a pension, assume that benefit erosion will continue.
- Assume you will work longer.
- Assume you will live longer.
- Assume that there will be unplanned challenges, both financial and nonfinancial.

Here's my definition of the Individual Retirement Attitude: I can no longer assume that any institution has my best interests at heart, and I will assume total responsibility for my fiscal well-being. I will plan on not only living longer but working longer as well, and I will be highly selective about the work I choose. I will remain flexible in my approach, as I know there will be surprises and challenges in the journey ahead.

Assume You Will Work Longer

We'll talk about this at length in the next two chapters. If indeed we buy into the idea that 65 is the new 55, or 45, or whatever chronological marker you choose, it also stands to reason that 65 would not necessarily be the date of extraction from the workforce. With ageist biases prevalent in many organizational settings, the pursuit and extension of work in your 60s and even early 70s will not be without its challenges. Maintaining relevance and up-to-speed aptitude in the modern workplace is the theme of Chapter 8.

Assume You Will Live Longer

How long should you plan on living? Should you consult an actuarial table or a longevity expert? I would recommend going with the expert—a recent study indicates that that expert is *you!*[1] The study explores Subjective Life Expectancy (SLE), a model where "individuals take into account their own age-related actuarial probabilities of life expectancy, but also consider other autobiographical details including factors such as their parents' longevity and their own lifestyles and health." In other words, we know ourselves better than anyone else. The research concluded that though the idea of SLE is a relatively new concept for research, there is enough evidence to conclude that self-estimates of life expectancy are reasonably accurate.

How long you expect to live has an important bearing on many of your "third stage of life" decisions—retirement being one of the first and foremost. Changes in Western societies demographically, economically, and socially have worked to form novel patterns for retirement. Staged or bridged retirements are becoming more common. Because of the confluence of increased longevity, the gradual eradication of mandatory retirement policies, and the macro shift toward personal financial responsibility in retirement, we will see these bridged retirements grow ever longer.

So based on your family DNA and your personal health habits/lifestyle, what is your best estimate for longevity? Your guess is as good as the actuarial experts. If you believe your expectancy to be 87, you can work backwards from that number with regard to both your financial and life satisfaction needs and begin to plot out your individual retirement path. SLE allows you to design your own time frame for how you will transition through retirement, as well as how you will plan the distribution of your finances through the various stages, which one author described as go-go, slow-go, and no-go.

Ask yourself the following questions:

- How old do I feel versus my actual age?
- What is my optimum "work until" age?
- What has been my parents'/grandparents' average longevity?
- How would I rate my dietary, physical fitness, and intellectual growth overall on a 1–10 scale?

From your answers to these questions, you can make a guesstimate at your own life expectancy. And keep in mind that how long you decide to work can have a bearing on this number as well. It would stand to reason that those who expect to live longer would also plan to retire later. A study by van Solinge and Henkens (2010) supported this assumption, showing that "Subjective Life Expectancy was a significant predictor of intended retirement age, even after controlling for important demographic factors such as gender, age, income, education, health, marital status, and family longevity."[2]

Another study by von Bonsdorff, Shultz, Leskinen, and Tansky found that those who expect to live longer may feel that they have time to engage in both work and nonwork activities. These people tend to see death as a far-off event relative to others of the same age. Because of this, they aren't ready to consider changing life priorities and retirement. They also concluded that those who have a high SLE are "likely to be contemplating a long retirement period with lots of opportunities for activity," and consequently will sense the need to be engaged in paid work for a longer period in order to be able to pay for the retirement that they envision.[3]

On the flip side, those late career workers with a short SLE would be inclined to avoid considering negative information about the financial risks of early retirement and would opt to focus instead on activities like leisure and family togetherness. Either way, it is left to you.

The bottom line is that our mental/attitudinal approach is a significant factor in this stage of life. Research results indicate that late career workers and retirees have "developed a mental model of their own likely life expectancy, and this mental model influenced decisions that have important consequences both for their personal circumstances as well as for organizations managing projected skill shortages and for governments planning for the social security of older people."[4]

As individuals, we are in charge of our own destinies more than we think. While there will always be unexpected, accidental, and unavoidable events, we're all better off determining our own paths instead of leaving the journey to institutions.

Assume That There Will Be Improvisational Challenges

As stated earlier, because it takes time for us to adjust both psychologically and financially to full retirement, bridges or transitions in and out of work have become more common. Postretirement bridge employment has positive implications for those organizations that seek to maintain talent and knowledge. In addition to the obvious financial gains, it also has physical and mental health benefits for us as individuals.

There are many already-retired persons who have returned to paid bridge employment. For over a decade there has been a growing body of research demonstrating that those who leave retirement to reenter the workforce have more positive attitudes to their preretirement work and are in better health. In other words, they feel healthy—both in body and spirit—and they know that by being engaged, they will extend that good health.

Chances are, if you attempt full retirement, you won't get it right the first time. As we've already discussed, it can take most of us two to four attempts to find the exact balance of the vocation and vacation we are searching for. It also takes time to find the proper balance between spending and saving. More time in play equals more spent and less earned. We will discuss this economic balance in more detail in Chapter 13.

Not surprisingly, two of the chief financial motivators for people who are engaged in bridge employment in their 60s and 70s are (1) medical health insurance and (2) being able to continue contributing to a workplace retirement plan, both of which increase in importance as we age.[5] Many of us, when considering inflationary health coverage and health care costs, decide that it is worth working longer to maintain coverage. Many of us want to delay distributions of our 401(k) plans, and so we continue to work and build those assets.

In the long run there are two balances you are challenged with finding on an individual level: working and playing and spending and saving. Allow yourself a practice run or two to find the balance you need. It is no longer necessary to think of retirement as a cliff to jump from (which is why people wanted parachutes) but as an uncharted road where you will need to advance carefully and map out what you like and don't like. There will be bridges in and out of employment, volunteer engagements, and more.

Consequently, modern retirement is a bit like an improvisational stage of life where you'll be deciding to go in and out of work and other interests based on how you feel at the time and how well balanced your current lifestyle feels to you. "Have fun with it" are the words of one practice-run retiree in her 70s who decided to leave the corporate world behind in her late 50s, start her own retail business, and dabble in a number of different ventures.

As you age and meet the improvisational challenges of this stage of life, you will find many that have blazed the trail ahead of you saying that "It is more about attitude than anything else." What is the healthiest outlook you can take into the next stage of life? The following are essential:

- *I will be a driver and not a passenger.* I will assume responsibility for my own well-being, financially and otherwise.
- *I will respond instead of despond.* I'm going to make the most of the situation I am in. If I need to go back to work, I'm going to look for work that has social and intellectual benefits.
- *I will thrive, not just survive.* With all the wisdom and experience I have gathered, I know what matters and what doesn't. I will apply that wisdom and direct my efforts in the most meaningful ways possible.

Viktor Frankl once wrote about the relationship between "position" and "disposition" and how understanding this distinction can make a difference in our lives. The difference, he taught, is that one state—position—is the situation we find ourselves in. We may not have planned it this way, but here we are. We now have a choice about how to respond to this position—disposition. Some choose to become bitter, dismayed, and angry that things didn't go according to plan. Others choose to take a position to enjoy the adventure of it all, rise to the challenges, explore new avenues, and revel in the novelty of new paths. Frankl taught that "position taken" is far more important than the position you find yourself in at the moment. This, in a nutshell, is what attitude is all about: figure out what position you are in, and determine what *position you will take!*

Individual Retirement Attitude

Knowing full well that the age of paternalistic pensions and institutional stewardship is past, I will assume the locus of control over my own retirement planning. If it is going to be positive, it will be up to me. I will accept all the correlating responsibilities of looking out for my own future.

CHAPTER 4

Money Is Only Part of the Equation

Many people are so occupied with getting out of a career trap that they seem to care little about what happens after they leave their jobs. Despite the fact they have planned other aspects of their lives, they seem to feel retirement will take care of itself. The opposite is often true.

—Elwood Chapman and Marion Haynes, authors,
Comfort Zones: Planning Your Future

I recently had a conversation with a man who has been involved in financial planning for over 30 years about would-be retirees' lack of preparedness on the advent of their transition. He said, "I ask the couple, 'What are you going to do in retirement?' And frequently I'm met with blank stares."

What difference will all our financial planning for the future make if we have no idea what kind of life we want to purchase with those finances?

Would you prepare for a two-week overseas vacation and not make any arrangements for how you will best use your time once you arrive? Only an intrepid adventurer or a cavalier fool would approach an expensive journey this way. Even just heading out for a short weekend trip, one may spend considerable time plotting out hotel, route, food, and entertainment options. Why, then, embark on a 30-year journey with the sole concern being economic?

Millions are saving for what might be a 35-year journey—with absolutely no idea where that journey might take them. Individuals who approach retirement in this manner will have a ticket to ride but no road map. While this may sound appealing, they may soon find themselves lost.

How important is it to you to have direction in the journey ahead? Existential preparation is more important than economic preparation if you plan on reaping enjoyment with the life ahead.

Money has no value in and of itself. Money is useful only in terms of what you can do with it. Just as important as saving for the future is having some sort of vision of what that future will be. Numbers crunching alone will not do the job. An inspiring vision of what you might be and do if you were financially able must accompany the numbers crunching if you hope to have a successful transition into whatever your next phase of life may be.

When I wrote the first edition of this book, the National Endowment for Financial Education had convened a think tank to discuss retirement planning.[1] The think tank was not limited to financial professionals but included gerontologists, researchers, a social worker, and a psychologist as well. Some of the touch points that these varied professionals developed included:

- The picture of retirement has changed dramatically and will continue to change.
- Consumers have become more responsible for the success or failure of their own retirement.
- The financial services industry is realizing it needs to do a much better job of educating the public about the features, possibilities, and parameters of this new retirement.

More than 10 years later, these touch points still matter. Although money is a primary concern in this new phase of life, it is just one of many. This report on the future of retirement planning stated, "Future retirees need to be asking what they want to do with their life during retirement, and what the personal implications of retirement are for them. Baby Boomers are looking for a meaningful role in their later adulthood. Money is important to them, but so is the quality of life in their retirement."

I am assuming, because you have read this far, that you have already settled in your mind some basic ideas about retirement, namely:

- Retirement at a predetermined age is an outdated concept.
- The age at which to retire or the decision to retire at all is based on inner desire and not outer resources.
- Work can and should be an expression of one's soul and a means for making a meaningful contribution to the world we live in.
- Much of the aging process hinges on choices we make regarding activity, involvement, and attitude.

Where from Here?

Alice came to a place where there were many roads. She stopped and asked the owl for directions. The owl asked, "Do you know where you want to go?"

Alice said, "No."

"Well then," the owl said, "it doesn't make any difference which path you take now."

—Lewis Carroll, *Alice in Wonderland*

Before you do the important work of crunching the numbers for the retirement stage of life, you'll want to crunch some numbers regarding life itself. I have prepared the Retirement Life Profile (Figures 4.1–4.4) for this purpose. In this profile, you have the opportunity to measure your approach to retirement life against four philosophical pillars of the New Retirementality: Vision, Balance, Work, and Successful Aging. In three of four of the following pillars you will see a number that quantitatively expresses your progress toward a life that will fulfill you in retirement.

I have developed these four pillars by identifying the most prevalent characteristics of successful or failed retirements:

1. *Vision* is important because successful retirees retire *to* something—failed retirees retire *from* something.
2. *Balance* is important because successful retirees find balance between vocation and vacation, and failed retirees go from bingeing on work to bingeing on leisure.

3. *Work* is important because successful retirees keep themselves plugged into meaningful pursuits, and failed retirees devolve into boredom and aimlessness.
4. *Successful Aging* is important because successful retirees focus on growing and well-being, and failed retirees just take what comes.

By completing this profile, you will begin laying the foundation for a healthier stage of life. My hope is that if you do retire, you will do so on purpose—with purpose. Perhaps you'll never fully retire because the word *retirement* will be eradicated from your vocabulary. As George Eliot said, "It's never too late to be what you might have been." Let's get started.

Visioning

> *I have come to the conclusion that more retirements will fail for non-financial reasons than for financial reasons.*
>
> —Michael Stein, author,
> *The Prosperous Retirement: Guide to the New Reality*

Don't think about retiring from something but instead to something. This thought has surfaced in my research as a hallmark of successful lives in retirement versus those that fail. Those who fail are thinking of retiring from something but have no clear vision of where they want to go—and end up being aimless. In fact, I'm not sure you should be thinking about completely retiring at all! While sipping martinis by the pool or playing golf five days a week may sound like a grand life right now, after a month or two, you might realize these are better as diversions than they are as lifestyles. I've heard from scores of people who thought they wanted a life of ease but instead got a life of boredom. Creating a vision of what you want the rest of your life to look like is a critical part of developing your New Retirementality.

Sit down with your partner: Each of you should select six pictures in the Vision exercise in Figure 4.1 and have a conversation around your personal vision of life. This exercise is simple and is intended to lead into a conversation with your spouse or partner, financial planner, life coach, or anyone else who may be helping you prepare for the next stage. Think about why you chose the pictures you did and how you plan on fulfilling those visions of life.

Visioning

*Our VISIONING PROCESS in the **24 Things to do in Retirement** exercise will help you get a clearer picture of what you want to experience in the rich years ahead.*

Directions: Choose 6 images (below) that fit your vision for retirement.

Figure 4.1 Visioning

Finding Balance

Did you know that every single person—from the multimillionaire to the person with few resources beyond Social Security—has the same amount to spend in retirement? All have exactly 168 hours per week in their account. No matter how much money people may have, if they do not have a plan for capitalizing on their time, they will not enjoy a fruitful stage of life.

Ever felt like life was just moving too fast? Ever felt like you just needed a little more time for your family or for yourself, to do absolutely nothing? I have found that many people who were workaholics their entire life find that they have forgotten how to enjoy themselves and how to live a life that balances work and play along with silence and activity.

We all need balance in our lives, whether we wake up each day thinking, "I can't believe I get paid to do this," or daydream about being a thousand miles away. While work may always be a part of our lives, we all need more. Taking time out to reconnect with our passions, enjoy a new experience, or spend time with family and friends is the yin to work's yang.

Living a balanced life leads to being a more balanced creature, which leads to being a pleasant person to be around. You may have to teach yourself how to live this way. The following exercise is a first step. Rather than jumping off the cliff of employment and hoping for a parachute to lead you to a safe landing, take a look at how you're spending your time now and what adjustments you would ultimately desire to make to order your life into a more tolerable pace.

Many people discover that a cold-turkey retirement is not the answer. They find themselves missing some of the activities and interactions and productive activities associated with work they did. What they really wanted was balance! Balance in work and play. Balance in family and personal time. Balance in running about and sitting still. Once this is achieved, life becomes quite exciting—in a more quiet way.

In this exercise, do your best to analyze your current allocation of 168 hours a week, and then fill in your desired life portfolio and compare the two. Examine what areas are crying out for time in your life and figure out the changes necessary to make those adjustments happen. This way, you can get a visual representation of the life you have and the life you want (see Figure 4.2).

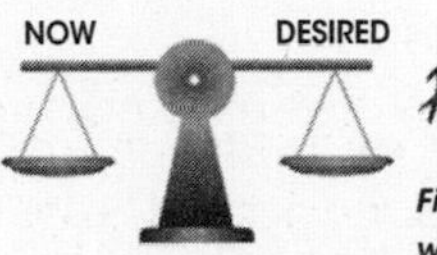

Finding Balance

Finding balance begins by becoming aware of exactly how and where we spend our time. Each of us has exactly 168 hours each week to manage.

CURRENT LIFE PORTFOLIO

Directions: Determine approximately how and where you ***currently*** spend your time. (Total must be 168 hours.)

	Hours/Week	% of Time
• Family/Friends		
• Work/Career		
• Downtime (t.v., surfing the web, music)		
• Sleep		
• Health/Fitness		
• Personal Growth (hobbies, learning a new skill)		
TOTAL:		

DESIRED LIFE PORTFOLIO

Directions: Determine approximately how and where you ***desire*** to spend your time. (Total must be 168 hours.)

	Hours/Week	% of Time
• Family/Friends		
• Work/Career		
• Downtime (t.v., surfing the web, music)		
• Sleep		
• Health/Fitness		
• Personal Growth (hobbies, learning a new skill)		
TOTAL:		

What allocations can I make with my time to bring more balance to my life?

(Max 1500 Characters)

Figure 4.2 Balance

Collecting a Playcheck

What you spend your life doing should be fulfilling to you—period. If it's not, you need to take responsibility and commit to making a change. How do you go from collecting a paycheck to collecting a *playcheck?* Life is simply too short to settle for a lukewarm existence. If you're not spending your time doing something you find fulfilling, it's time for a career assessment and transformation. If you are looking toward retiring, you'll want to address the need for the expression of work, to some degree, in your life ahead. While most people don't conduct a work assessment before retiring, a high percentage end up taking on part-time work within the first year because they realize they were missing out on positive aspects of work.

In this exercise, you have the opportunity to compare your working situation against the seven factors of fulfillment at work: (1) how well your talents and abilities are utilized, (2) your enthusiasm level toward your work, (3) how much fulfillment you derive from the work you do, (4) the quality of the people you work with, (5) the growth you experience as a result of your work, (6) the benefit to others that is created through your work, and (7) the degree that you are energized by what you do.

The last part of this exercise asks you to cooperatively rank the work you do with the pay you receive. The worst possible ranking is a combination of hating your work and receiving terrible pay, while the best possible ranking is absolutely loving your work and not believing you're actually getting paid what you are to do what you do. Most people fall somewhere in between.

With introspection, guidance, and persistence, you can find work that will reward you with a playcheck. The exercise in Figure 4.3 will help you determine how close you are right now.

From Aging to S-Aging

The final cornerstone in preparing to succeed for the rest of your life is to shift from simply aging (getting old) to successful aging (what I like to call "s-aging"). When I asked Mary, a 96-year-old dancer from a local dance studio, how she did it, she told me she just never stopped, but instead kept moving forward. I heard the same answer from a 70-something man shooting baskets at the local gym.

These people and others like them are examples of *retirementors*—they show us how to live with vitality and vigor for the rest of our lives. People stay young in mind, body, and spirit by staying active in mind, body, and spirit.

Successful aging is all about attitude. I'll bet you know someone who is 80 years old but acts like they are half their age, and vice versa, someone who is 40 and acts like they're 80. You're old when you think you are. S-aging is all about knowing what it takes to keep going—both mentally and physically—by challenging yourself every day of your life. Just because you're not 20 years old doesn't mean you can't be curious, challenged, connected, creative, and

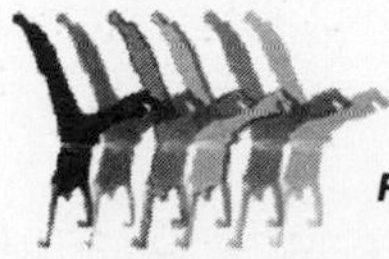

Collecting a Playcheck

Find work that unites your head, your heart, and your hands.

Directions: On a scale from 1 to 5, rate yourself on your true level of contentment - 1 being "Not content" and 5 being "Completely content".

	1	2	3	4	5
1. I feel as though my natural talents and abilities are expressed through my work.	O	O	O	O	O
2. I have a continuing enthusiasm about the work I do.	O	O	O	O	O
3. I have a sense of serenity regarding my work.	O	O	O	O	O
4. I enjoy the people I work with.	O	O	O	O	O
5. I feel my work helps me to grow intellectually and personally.	O	O	O	O	O
6. I feel that I bring some benefit to others through my work.	O	O	O	O	O
7. I often feel energized by the work I do.	O	O	O	O	O

Directions: Read the ten statements below and decide which one best describes how you currently feel about your job and pay. Then, click the corresponding number on the graphic below.

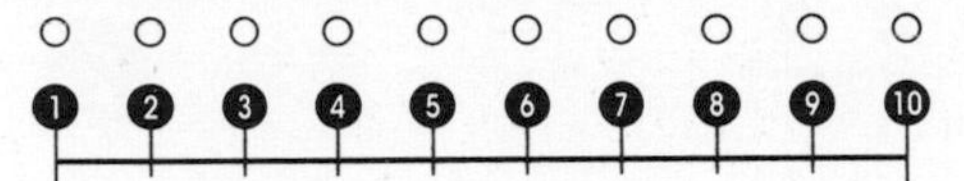

1. I dread my work and the pay is terrible.
2. I dread my work but the pay is decent.
3. I hate this work but the pay is excellent.
4. This work is okay but the pay isn't good.
5. This work is okay and the pay is okay as well.
6. This work is okay and the pay is excellent.
7. This work is great but the pay isn't.
8. This work is great and the pay is okay.
9. This work is great and the pay is excellent.
10. I'm having a blast and can't believe I get paid this kind of money to do it!

TOTAL [ ]

SCORING KEY

8–17 You are collecting a paycheck
18–24 Danger zone—change may be needed
25–35 You're on your way to a playcheck
36–45 Congratulations! You are collecting a "playcheck"!

Figure 4.3 Playcheck

charitable. All it takes is the right mind-set. S-aging is about thriving, not just surviving.

In the following exercise, you can rate your lifestyle against the "Vitamin Cs of Successful Aging" and then review some short tips on boosting your Vitamin Cs (see Figure 4.4).

From Aging to S-Aging

"Aging reflects the relationship of time on our being. Aging describes, in large part, the state of our body. Old, on the other hand, describes our state of mind. It has always been a matter of great interest to me to discover the spiritual and attitudinal aquifer that supplies the fountain of youth." —Mitch Anthony

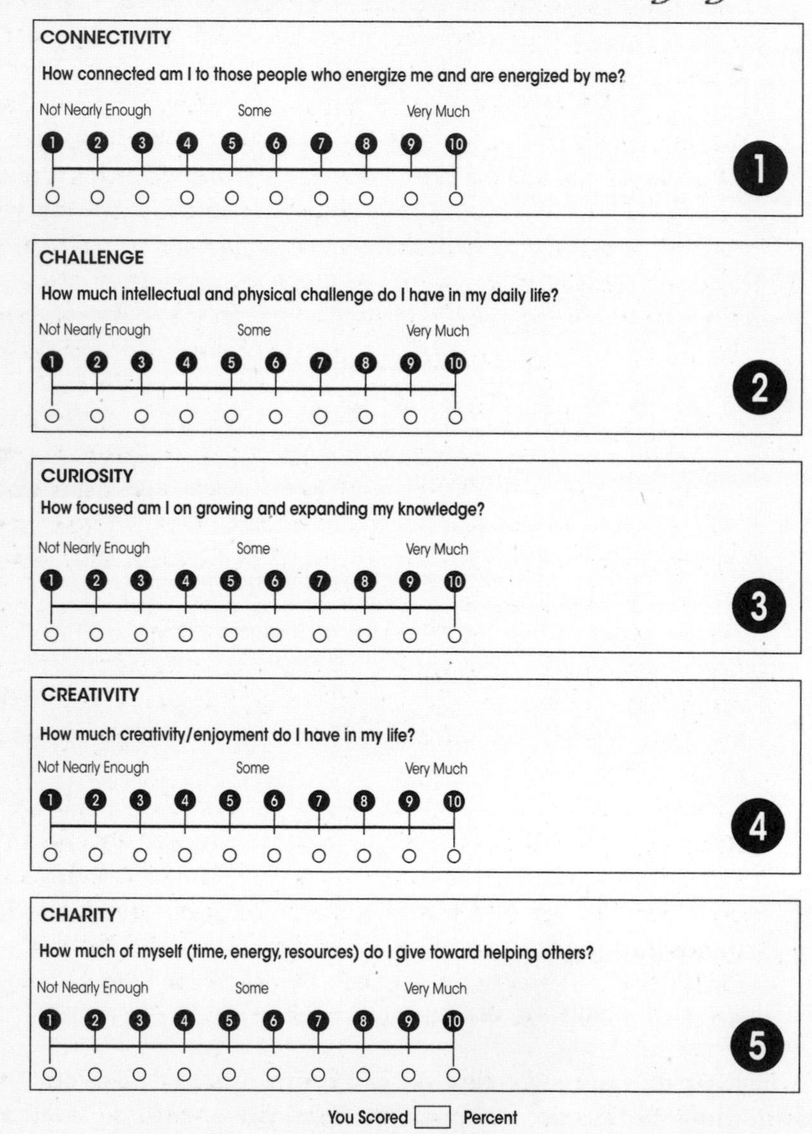

The 5 Attitudes of Successful Aging

CONNECTIVITY

How connected am I to those people who energize me and are energized by me?

Not Nearly Enough — Some — Very Much

1 2 3 4 5 6 7 8 9 10

1

CHALLENGE

How much intellectual and physical challenge do I have in my daily life?

Not Nearly Enough — Some — Very Much

1 2 3 4 5 6 7 8 9 10

2

CURIOSITY

How focused am I on growing and expanding my knowledge?

Not Nearly Enough — Some — Very Much

1 2 3 4 5 6 7 8 9 10

3

CREATIVITY

How much creativity/enjoyment do I have in my life?

Not Nearly Enough — Some — Very Much

1 2 3 4 5 6 7 8 9 10

4

CHARITY

How much of myself (time, energy, resources) do I give toward helping others?

Not Nearly Enough — Some — Very Much

1 2 3 4 5 6 7 8 9 10

5

You Scored ☐ **Percent**

Figure 4.4 Vitamin Cs of Successful Aging

Tips on Boosting Your Vitamin Cs of Successful Aging

- *Stay connected* to people and places you enjoy. Be sure your New Retirementality plan includes living and working in a place and environment that won't disconnect you from family, friends, or activities that are important to you. Think beyond traditionally planned communities or destinations to cities, both large and small, college and university towns, places that support the arts, and areas that are easily accessible to sporting activities you enjoy. There are probably one or two places that are within close proximity to family and friends, making it possible to have the best of both worlds.
- *Challenging yourself* doesn't have to involve climbing Mount Everest. Think about simple things you can do to keep your mental acuity alive. If you've never picked up a paintbrush, take a watercolor class. If you love crossword puzzles, try Sudoku. If you've never taught, be a mentor to someone. Challenge yourself enough to learn and have fun at the same time, but not so much that you get frustrated and quit.
- *Curiosity* is what keeps you growing. Be open to learning new things and committed to growing your awareness. Start a conversation with the person next to you or learn about a culture or religion you're unfamiliar with. Active mental activity is as crucial to your emotional health as it is your physical well-being.
- *Being creative* doesn't apply only to the arts. Explore your passion—whether it's fixing cars, rearranging furniture, or keeping a diary. Being creative means being intrigued, expressive, and intentional—in other words, passionate and interested in life.
- Giving to others is the greatest gift we can give to ourselves. *Being charitable* doesn't have to cost a cent and shouldn't be a burden—volunteer to tutor an at-risk student, help someone learn to read, open the door for someone with their hands full—these are all ways to be charitable. Even if you didn't live a day longer because of your charitable acts, you no doubt will have lived a much richer life.

The final chapter in this book, "From Aging to S-aging," will cover these factors in more depth and will encourage you with ideas you can adopt for a more successful aging process.

If you have prepared well financially, you will have more opportunities to make choices about vision, balance, enjoyable work, and lifestyle. Money is always a part of the equation but is not the whole equation. If you are not prepared financially, do not despair. You can still tweak aspects of your lifestyle, your working life, and your general sense of balance. Money is not the cure-all. As one retired gentleman put it to me, "All I was ever told was save for retirement, save for retirement. So I did. No one ever told me prepare for the rest of your life. What am I supposed to do now? Sit around and hug my checkbook?"

I could see in his eyes that he regretted not spending more time contemplating life after the retirement transition. Once we make that transition, that is what we are left with—a life either fulfilling or not.

The opportunity for emotional shortsightedness often crops up with the person suddenly facing real retirement prospects. What we once called retirement—because those who retired stopped working—we now see as a life transition to other work, less work, or very little work. Both money issues and emotional issues accompany this transition and need to be dealt with. Whether you engage professional help or do it on your own, it is vital to your future to recognize that retirement is not just an economic event. If you do choose to retire, financial preparation becomes just one aspect of a life event. Your life ledger is more important than your retirement fund.

Keep this in mind and you won't get caught in the retirement whiplash that has surprised so many people. Next, we will visit how to make the transition with the least amount of shock and turbulence.

Individual Retirement Attitude

- Make plans to occupy your mind, time, and energies in retirement.
- Do all you can to maintain personal health and well-being.
- Decide how you will define success once your financial goals are met.

CHAPTER 5

Retirement Whiplash: Be Careful of What You Wish For

"If you think going to the moon is hard, try staying at home."
—Astronaut Barbara Ceman

r.e.t.i.r.e.d.
tired-er
r.e.t.r.i.e.d

I wish I had a dollar for every time I asked a retirement-age person, "Are you retired?" and they replied, "I was but flunked the course." Or "I tried but failed at retirement." Ralph Steiner, who sold his financial planning practice in 2007 and is now running a succession planning company casually tells people that he flunked retirement and decided to help other advisors do what he did—find something to do with the rest of their lives. This is not an uncommon situation today.

Two British groups, the Institute of Economic Affairs think tank and the Age Endeavour Fellowship charity, released a report assessing whether retirement had a negative impact on people's health.[1] Gabriel Sahlgren, the author of the study, says it's a no-brainer that people do diminish physically as a result of an unfulfilling retirement. Sahlgren notes that the longer people have been retired, the less likely they are to rate their own health as good, the more likely they are to have a diagnosed medical problem, and the more likely they are to be suffering from clinical depression.

Sahlgren believes the inactivity and inertia that often accompanies retirement is a significant contributor to the problem. He has taken the point of view that raising the retirement age (a process that Britain's current government has hastened in that country) would be a good policy remedy to this problem, stating that "later retirement should, in fact, lead to better average health in retirement."

Unexpected Segues

Research released by the nonprofit Transamerica Center for Retirement Studies® underscores how American workers are largely unprepared for retirement and how relatively few have a backup plan in the event they are forced into retirement earlier than planned. The Annual Transamerica Retirement Survey—conducted among 4,080 American workers—found that for many Americans, the foundation of their retirement strategy is simply to not retire or to work considerably longer than the traditional retirement age of 65. Almost 40 percent (39 percent) of American workers plan to retire after age 70 or not at all, and over half (54 percent) of workers plan to work in retirement.

While many of us may plan to work past the traditional retirement age or never retire, unforeseen circumstances could force us to stop working sooner than we planned. The survey found the majority of respondents are unprepared for this scenario—70 percent agree they could work until age 65 and still not have enough money saved to meet their retirement needs. This sentiment spans across age and income.

People are often forced into retirement before they are ready. Others think they are ready, and yet are not prepared for the existential realities of the condition known as retirement. Here are some of the common reasons why retirees were pushed toward retirement earlier than expected:

- 51 percent: health problems or disability
- 21 percent: downsizing or closure
- 19 percent: having to care for a spouse or other family member
- 11 percent: changes in skills for job requirement
- 23 percent: other

A common circumstance for those thrust unwittingly into retirement is that they are suddenly left to negotiate with a loss of structure in their lives. Jobs can offer structure that is perceived both positively and negatively. As one sudden retiree put it, "What am I going to do now? I knew I was ready to retire, but I didn't know what I would do. Would I sleep 'til noon and eat candy all day or what?"

This particular retiree joined a retiree peer education group to restore some structure into her life and felt that it not only reinstated structure but also kept her mind alert. She said she thought the participation saved her life.

Another retiree echoed this loss of structure as disorientating. This individual noted that once he retired, he achieved freedom but found that often no one seemed to realize he even existed. He experienced an existential void wondering daily if he mattered anymore. This is not a rare sentiment but one I have been told over and over again during the past decade of studying this condition of having retirement thrust upon one's state of being.

Sudden Retirement Syndrome

In addition to difficulties relating to lack of preparedness, sudden retirees are in the often unwelcome position of having to redefine themselves.

—Susan K. Bradley, CFP, author, *Sudden Money*

If you want to get an accurate picture of what retirement might feel like, it is better to learn from someone who has been suddenly retired at an early age, as opposed to learning about it from someone who worked for 40 years in a job he didn't particularly like and then retired at 65. Sudden retirees are those who ended up in a retired state because of unexpected events such as the merger or sale of a business, downsizing, injury, sickness, caregiving for a family member, or the death of a breadwinning spouse. The experiences of these individuals might be a better looking glass for previewing some of your concerns in the early phases of retirement. Many of the people who have been cast into unexpected retirements are often still young at heart, energetic, and full of vision for their future—this description may apply to you, regardless of your age.

Sudden retirees find themselves having to make many life decisions before they are ready. Ideally, we want to learn how to live within our activity needs and financial limits before we reach the retirement stage of life. We hear and read plenty on the financial aspects but not as much on the activity and existence ledgers of life. One study I read found that many people articulate that they are merely "resigned to their retirement" as opposed to truly being satisfied with it.

Over a decade ago when I first began theorizing that the full story wasn't being told around retirement I was quite amazed at what I learned in research, both formally established and empirically confirmed again and again. What I discovered were the four Ds and the Big B of retirement: Death, Divorce, Disability, Drunkenness, and Boredom. Today's research confirms these patterns. I remember research from a generation ago from IBM demonstrating that their average retiree didn't make it to his 24th pension check! While longevity rates have increased, I still hear stories about people who retire and die within a year's time.

I'm convinced that there are two specific reasons this happens. One is that the individual literally worked himself to death by burning the candle at both ends and retiring into his final decline. The story I hear more often, however, is the person who wakes up on day 32 of retirement and realizes she has no specific purpose, plan, or meaning. These are the individuals who die of aimlessness.

In a cohort study of thousands of employees who worked at Shell Oil, investigators found that embarking on the retirement path at age 55 doubled the risk for death before reaching age 65, compared with those who toiled beyond age 60:

> "Failing health might have played a role in the younger retirees' higher mortality," said Shan P. Tsai, Ph.D., an epidemiologist at Shell Health Services, according to the report in the *British Medical Journal.* Dr. Tsai and his colleagues challenged the notion that early retirement means less stress and a more relaxed lifestyle which has fueled the belief that retiring young boosts longevity. Their results indicate the opposite: *Mortality rates improved with an older retirement age.*[2]

Freakonomics

The trend toward working longer because of economic necessity may feel discouraging to you at the moment, but it's important to consider the upside of this predicament. The economist Josef Zweimuller at the University of Zurich recently coauthored a study that found that even though many crave early retirement, it seems to be bad for our health: "[A]mong blue-collar workers, we see that workers who retire earlier have a higher mortality rates and these effects are pretty large."

The study showed that for every extra year of early retirement, workers lost about two months of life expectancy. Other researchers, including University of Florida psychologist Mo Wang, who studies retirement, and Steve Levitt, author of the bestseller *Freakonomics*, have found the same phenomena around earlier retirement. Levitt has personally settled on a plan to retire *and* keep working at the same time.

Welcome to the real world of retirement. In an article for CBS Money Watch, Steve Vernon made a commentary on the RP-2000 Mortality Study, which included a table that compared the annual death rates among two groups of men aged 50 to 70. The first group consisted of men who were working, and the second group included men who were fully retired. The death rates of those who were still working were roughly half that of the death rates of men the same age who were fully retired. "What's going on here?" Vernon wrote, "I thought retirement was supposed to be good for you!"[3]

Does working actually enable you to live longer, or is it simply correlative with no direct cause from work? An example explanation that was offered on the correlative side of the argument is that people who are in poor health and disabled would fall into the retired group, whereas only healthy people can continue to work. But this argument doesn't hold water, as those on disability benefits and those in failing health were excluded from the study.

There are numerous longitudinal studies and plenty of anecdotal evidence appearing on the side of work being a causative factor in longevity. George Vaillant's book *Aging Well* summarized this evidence in detail. A vital engagement with life is a primary factor in prolonging life. You can get engagement with life from working, but you can also get it from taking up causes, volunteering, pursuing hobbies, and contributing to your family and community. Vernon's conclusion on the matter was: "Here's the takeaway for me: Finding powerful reasons for getting up in the morning in my retirement years is as important as my financial planning. We may need to work a little in our retirement years to make ends meet. In this case, I won't be bitter—working may be keeping me alive!"

Amen, brother. That's the attitude required.

For Better or Worse but Not for Lunch

I once met a wonderful financial planner in New Jersey who told me that one of the most heartbreaking scenarios that kept being repeated in his planning practice was clients divorcing upon retirement. With sadness he talked about how discouraging it was to spend years assisting these couples (whom he had grown quite fond of) breaking apart upon retirement. This is not what they had planned for, but the lesson that proper spacing is required for relationships to last can fall hard in the retirement transition. This particular planner told me that, as a preemptive move to prepare them better for the transition, he started sending this book to them a year ahead of their proposed retirement date.

My mother in law preempted any such development in her marriage when she sat down with her husband on the first day of his retirement from teaching math for 42 years and asked him to sign a document she had drafted called "The Pre-retirement Agreement." The agreement was literally Prenup Meets Retirement! One woman in Texas put it to me in colloquial math terms: "I've got twice the husband, half the space—and he's getting bigger." It's hard to top that description, and I know it resonates with a lot of spouses.

In 1990, approximately 206,000 people aged 50 and older got divorced, whereas in 2010, about 643,150 got divorced. By 2030, it's estimated that the number of persons divorced could reach more than 820,000 for ages 50 and above. The rate of divorce is highest for those who are unemployed (21.2 divorced per 1,000 married persons) than for those who are employed either full or part time (12.4 and 10.0 divorced per 1,000 married persons, respectively).[4]

The 19th Hole

My friend Larry told me about a friend of his who was the envy of his peers when he took full retirement at age 55 and headed to Florida to pursue a life of golfing leisure. After serendipitously running into his old pal seven years later, he said to me, "We're exactly the same age, but to look at us you'd swear there were 15 years between us—my friend being on the not-so-flattering end of the comparison." His friend confided to him over dinner that his dream of 18 holes a day had become "stalled at the 19th hole and might explain some things." This man had been a mover and shaker in his industry and complained that now "he couldn't get a plumber to show up and felt he had been moved from 'Who's Who' to 'Who's he?'"

Role transitions theory purports that one's identification with preretirement employment roles will affect postretirement adjustment.[5] Maintenance of an individual's identity through the retirement process will lead to a better sense of well-being. Depending on the level of stress the preretirement role caused, role transitions can be experienced as either a relief or a loss.[6] Drinking can therefore increase or decrease, depending on whether alcohol use is associated with work-oriented social roles or whether alcohol is used to cope with role loss.

One study explored the impact of voluntariness of retirement—whether it was the individual's decision at the time—as a factor of retirement's impact on health outcomes. The authors concluded that both voluntary and involuntary retirees may use alcohol to cope with the stress of sudden change in their employment status.[7] High preretirement job satisfaction, involuntary retirement, and preretirement workplace stress are all risk factors for higher consumption of alcohol and a greater likelihood of alcohol problems. Retirement, for many, can mean diminished breadth of social roles, which can lead to discouragement. On the other side, individuals whose social circles increase during retirement may be at risk for problem drinking if those social influences are permissive of drinking. In the case of Larry's friend, the golf group's congregating all afternoon at the 19th hole was just such an influence.

Disability

I was surprised when I learned how great a percentage of retirees are in this phase as a result of a disability that prevented them from pursuing their original or desired work agenda. On a recent golf trip with an acquaintance, a physician, who had recently been diagnosed with an inoperable brain tumor, detailed for me how rough the transition *out of work* was for him. He was having trouble structuring his days and challenging his mind in the transition. At the end of 2012, almost 9 million wage earners in the United States (over 5 percent of the workforce) received Social Security disability benefits. Approximately 19 million Americans in their traditional working years (18–65) are disabled but not necessarily permanently. The Council for Disability Awareness published the following samples illustrating the odds of disability by gender:

- A typical female, age 35, 5′4″, 125 pounds, nonsmoker, who works mostly an office job, with some outdoor physical responsibilities, and who leads a healthy lifestyle has a 24 percent chance of becoming disabled for 3 months or longer during her working career, with a 38 percent chance that the disability would last 5 years or longer, and with the average disability for someone like her lasting 82 months.
- A typical male, age 35, 5′10″, 170 pounds, nonsmoker, who works an office job, with some outdoor physical responsibilities, and who leads a healthy lifestyle has a 21 percent chance of becoming disabled for three months or longer during his working career, with a 38 percent chance that the disability would last 5 years or longer, and with the average disability for someone like him lasting 82 months.

If you are concerned with health issues preventing or truncating your work life expectations, you can assist your own shelf life by paying close attention to the factors that impel and impede disability. There are matters like traumatic injury or sudden or chronic health crises that one may have to endure that may not preventable, but also there are many conditions that emerge or are prolonged by lifestyle or health maintenance conditions.

Some of the factors that increase the risk of disability include excess body weight, tobacco use, high-risk activities or behaviors, chronic conditions such as diabetes, high blood pressure, back pain, anxiety or depression, and frequent alcohol consumption or substance abuse. Factors that decrease the risk of disability include maintaining a healthy body weight, no tobacco use, healthy diet and sleep habits, regular exercise, moderate to no alcohol consumption, avoidance of high-risk behaviors including substance abuse, maintaining a healthy stress level, and effective treatment of chronic health conditions.

Bore-dumb

I met "Fred" when he was 80 years old, and he looked and comported himself like a man 20 years his junior. At the time, he was running a nonprofit organization and working six- to eight-hour days. It was obvious in talking to him that retirement was an option he could choose any time he wanted—he just didn't want to. I asked what it was about retirement that failed to attract him.

He told me about turning 65 and all his close friends moving in pack to Palm Springs (the "last stop," he called it) to take up a life of retirement leisure. "They invited me out to sell me on the lifestyle, so I went to see. We sat down for cocktails before dinner, and each of them went around and told me about their golf match or tennis match stroke by stroke. The next year they invited me out again and told me they were going to "close the deal" with me. We sat down for cocktails (somewhat earlier than last year), and they went around the table one by one and told me about their golf and tennis matches stroke by stroke. And that's when I knew it. . . ."

He had me. "Knew what?" I asked.

"First you're bored, then you're boring," he concluded, "and I never want to be that boring." I laughed uproariously at his candor and incisiveness. I'd never heard anything like it, but I'll never forget how convincing he was as a relevant force at the age of 80. He instantly became one of my "retirementors." I want to have that kind of balance and relevance in my life as long as I possibly can. I love to play as much as the next guy, but I don't want to bore people with stories and accounts that put them to sleep because playing is all I have to do.

New Directions is an organization founded by Dave Corbett, author of *Portfolio Life*. Corbett believes that senior executives and professionals need specialized and customized help in navigating career transitions. His organization has developed a process to help clients identify their individual assets, needs, motivations, and goals, and then uses the results to craft action plans and explore new opportunities. Their clients are leaders in business—the professionals of academia and philanthropy and the fields from professional sports to public service—who are facing a significant life or work transition. Their approach guides people toward career and life paths aligned with their core values, talents, and interests—in short, with who they are. They help their clients find both employment and creative, meaningful ways to live life beyond a full-time job.

I love this copy that I read on the New Directions web site:

> People now recognize that the second half of life can mean a second wind—and not just a breeze but a gust to fill our sails. It is a time in life to contribute, learn and try new things. But the bonus of extended middle age is still so new that many discover that they failed to plan adequately for it.

> Many retired people feel busy, but too often it's busy about things that don't cut to the quick of our lives. Maybe that's why studies show that 50 percent of retirees are bored.
>
> "I left my company with no plan and no goals," said one former senior manager at a computer company who soon found himself adrift. He described his planning process like this: "Retirement looks great . . . So far so good . . . Now, wait a minute, I'm getting a little antsy . . . Oops, what have I done?"

This client did get ready financially to retire, but he didn't plan new goals to replace those of his career. He assumed that retirement would take care of itself.

The Oops Factor; Rearview Mirror

Like this retired executive, many of us walk into retirement with rose-colored glasses and naïveté regarding the impact on our emotional, social, intellectual, and spiritual beings. We must enter with eyes wide open to the dangers, pitfalls, and traps that swallow many whole, and from which many never return.

How do you avoid the deleterious impact of retirement? How can you and your friends avoid the undesirable condition of retirement whiplash, where the reality catches up with you all of a sudden? I suggest having a conversation with your friends about work, intellectual capital, and the things all of you do to fuel personal esteem and expression. You might find many a willing participant for this discussion in the professional ranks. Age has nothing to do with it. It's all about what we bring to the game and how long we want to play. There's nothing wrong with going from being a starting player to a role player in the next phase of life, just as long as we are somewhat in the game while we have game.

I love going down to the local gym and shooting baskets and often see another gentleman shooting as well. One day we fell into a conversation about how much we enjoyed staying active in basketball. I mentioned that I hoped to be able to shoot baskets when I was 80. He told me he was 68 years old and said, "I'll tell you the key. It's very simple: *don't ever quit.* I've watched a lot of people use little pains as excuses, and when they tried to take it up later, it was too hard." I looked at him; he looked limber, much younger than his age, and fluid in his motion, and I knew he was right. No extended time completely out of the game for me. No time to think up excuses. I enjoy this too much.

Even if you're forced into the retirement predicament, don't ever quit on your intellectual, social, or spiritual advancements in life. You won't risk suffering whiplash if you can avoid the sudden braking on your personal growth and development by reaching for all the life you can get. The Transamerica Center for Retirement Studies offers the following recommendations to improve your long-term retirement outlook:

- Take on a part-time job while looking for full-time employment. This will help cover expenses and alleviate the need to take on more debt or dip into your retirement savings.
- Continuously update your job skills so you stay current—and relevant—with employers.
- Seek additional education and training.

You need to focus on what's ahead of you, not what's behind. Keep your eyes off the rearview mirror of life and the GPS—and focus on the road ahead. If you do so, you could find yourself living out a reality like Bill Glaccum, who turned 90 years young in June 2013. A member of the greatest generation, he served in the Navy in WWII. After returning to civilian life after the war, Bill decided to become a chiropractor. To support himself while studying to become a chiropractor, Bill was a dance instructor in the evenings at the Arthur Murray Dance Studio. He had a successful chiropractic practice in Atlanta for more than half a century. A few years ago, his son took over the practice, but Bill still works at the clinic every Wednesday. Spending an entire day adjusting patients is tiring, even for a young man, but Bill still puts in a full day once a week, even though he has started his tenth decade on Earth. He says the workout he gets from chiropractic work keeps him in shape for his twice-weekly golf game. Bill is also incredibly gregarious, and his workday enables him to keep in touch with patients who have also become friends over the decades.

Bill's story was sent to me by his financial planner, Mark Giovanni, CFP, who says Bill was his sponsor when he joined the local Rotary Club in 1996. He is also still Mark's chiropractor. Bill, inspired by Mark's life vision, has concluded, "I love the work I do as a CFP and head of my own business, and I have no desire to retire until I'm so addle-minded that no one will trust me with their money anymore. Bill is one of the reasons I feel confident that no age is too old to do what you love, especially if you are serving others in the process."

And there we have both the punch line and the cure for retirement whiplash: *it is finding a way to serve others.* Beautiful things appear and happen in the lives of those of who are looking to bring value to others. There is no time to feel sorry for ourselves while contemplating new ways to be useful. We don't have time to wallow while searching for opportunity. We don't have to wrestle with idleness when time is spoken for with meaningful activities. When we are searching, seeking, and serving others, meaning comes to us in abundance. Let's keep the pedal to the metal.

Individual Retirement Attitude

The most important consideration for me as I contemplate life in "retirement" is the state of my being, my heart and mind. Rather than opening the door to idleness, aimlessness, and languor, I will approach this as a time to challenge myself and open up new horizons.

The Retirement that Works

"Just as iron rusts from disuse, even so does inaction spoil the intellect."

—Leonardo Da Vinci

In the Industrial Age, *work* became a four-letter word, saddled with the baggage of soulless tasks and exploitive industrialists. In the Modern Age, where the majority of us trade intellectual, relational, and experiential capital toward a paycheck, the very definition of work is going through a revival. We are squarely in a renaissance period in the evolution of what work means to our lives. In many ways we find ourselves in our work. We discover who we are and who we are not. We discover our strengths and weaknesses, but also at a deeper level we find affirmation of our purpose on this planet and of our potential to positively impact others.

In *Man's Search for Meaning*, Viktor Frankl states that each of our lives resembles the work of a sculptor who chips away everything that is not, to reveal what is. Our work, in many respects, is a process of chipping away at the things that we are not to discover who we are. We are literally hammering out our values to someday reveal the absolute best form that we can become. We can no longer afford to gloss over or ignore this core discussion for the next generation of "retirees," which are so-called for lack of a better term. We are, in fact, "searchers" or "remodelers" of our own lives more than anything else.

An irrefutable fact of our times is the potential collision at the junction of life where retirement intersects with our need/desire for work. I have had the privilege of participating in this meaningful discussion with literally thousands of retirees and contemplators of retirement through the publication of the three previous editions of this book and the hundreds of public presentations it has opened up to me. The discussion continues to expand in our culture and will no doubt become *the* key discussion regarding retirement in the decade ahead. A trend portending in this direction is the recent proliferation of "retirement coaches." As people seek to carve out a meaningful existence in the expanding middle-age years, they are seeking wisdom and direction regarding what specific role work will play in that existence.

Reinventing Retirement—New Pathways

The reasons we have different attitudes toward retirement these days are manifold. A confluence of economic events, generational observations of others who were retired, and personal reexaminations of what is meaningful in our lives has led us to the place we now are—a place of discarding outdated assumptions around retirement. As Figure 6.1 illustrates, the reinvention of retirement was inevitable based on our personal experiences with the institution combined with changes in personal lifestyles, personal economies, and the economy at large.

Immersed in this discussion for over a decade, I have closely followed the yearly studies on retirement trends, opinions, and preparation. One annual study conducted in 2012 by the Transamerica

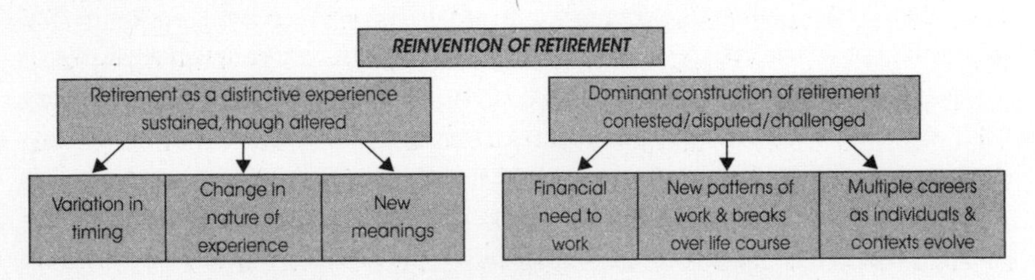

Figure 6.1 Reinvention of Retirement

Source: Leisa D. Sargent, Mary Dean Lee, Bill Martin, and Jelena Zikic, "Reinventing Retirement: New Pathways, New Arrangements, New Meanings," *Human Relations* 66, no. 1 (2013): 19. Copyright © 2013 by SAGE Publications. Reprinted by permission of SAGE.

Center for Retirement Studies proposed the following definition of *retirement readiness:*

> A state in which an individual is well prepared for retirement, should it happen as planned or unexpectedly, and can continue generating adequate income to cover living expenses throughout his/her lifetime through retirement savings and investments, employer pension benefits, government benefits, and/or continuing to work in some manner while allowing for leisure time to enjoy life.[1]

I find it interesting that work is now included in their latest definition of retirement. That reinforces the idea that "retirement" has now become an oxymoron—the latest generation to enter this phase of life that has made it so. Retirement is no longer a ledge of work we dive off, while hoping our parachute is sufficient. Retirement is no longer an age marker where we have to hope shuffleboard and early bird specials will fill our life expectations.

Modern retirees have no patience with stereotypes about aging—they are redefining retirement living. According to several studies, decisions are becoming more focused on social implications and intellectual stimulation, dispelling traditional myths that retirees are interested only in leisure activities. The new definition of retirement overwhelmingly advocated by today's retiree is one that emphasizes activity and engagement over leisure and rest. About 70 percent of those aged 50 to 75 (both retired and not yet retired) who were surveyed said they viewed retirement as "a time to begin a new chapter in life by being active and involved, starting new activities, and setting new goals." Retirement is a time to break out of the cocoon, not go into one. Only 28 percent of those in this age group preferred the definition offered by traditional retirement as "a time to take it easy, take care of yourself, enjoy leisure activities, and take a much-deserved rest from work and responsibilities."

It is important to note the diversity of the group that embraces this new definition. It appeals equally to men and women, liberals and conservatives, all regions of the country, people in their 50s as well as those in their 70s, people who are limited by physical or medical conditions and those who are not. It is an especially appealing definition to the better-educated and higher-income seniors. Fifty-six percent of those with a high school education chose the new definition of retirement, whereas 73 percent of those with a college education chose the same. The Hart study put it this way, "The better-educated and more affluent older Americans seem to express with even greater intensity a desire to continue to find new challenges in retirement to supplement their hard-sought professional identities."

One way many are incarnating this new definition is by refusing to leave the workplace altogether. They see it as the glue that guarantees an active and challenging life. Forty-two percent of nonretired people aged 50 to 75 report that they plan to work either part time or full time, or part time at another job after retiring from their main job. Currently, almost one in five older Americans who are retired from their principal career continue to work at another job. This number will rise steadily in the next 10 to 20 years. According to a 2013 Gallup poll, nearly three quarters of workers who have not yet retired report that they plan to work into their retirement years or never retire.[2] Forty percent are choosing to continue working to stay active and involved, while a smaller percentage (35 percent) need to for financial reasons.

Traditional retirement was premised only on wants, and society assumed that all retirees wanted were lives of leisure. The New Retirementality is premised on balancing needs and wants. Traditional retirement was focused on vacation, whereas the New Retirementality is focused on balancing *vocation* and *vacation.*

Retirement Planning that Works

Retirement is wonderful
If you have two essentials:
Much to live for, and
Much to live on.

—Anonymous

The discussion is expanding to the point that those claiming to be "retirement specialists" will need to become subspecialists in work theory and be able to provide some direction and education in this arena, which is key to our fulfillment in life. I have a very simple theory on the evolutionary role of work in our lives. What I mean by *evolutionary* is that our relationship toward work matures as we spend more time in the workplace. Clearly, we are not the same worker at 40 that we were at 25, and we are certainly not the same worker at 60 that we were at 40. Hopefully, as Frankl put it, we have chipped away large chunks of who we are not and are looking at a more vivid relief of who we really are as we enter our middle years.

To help understand the role of work in the various stages of life, we'll start with a broadened definition of work, and discuss the role work plays in our lives. Here's how I define work:

> An engagement that brings value to others and meaning to me.

Note that this definition does not exclude work to compensatory activities. Volunteerism is included if the activity is valuable to others and meaningful to you. At the same time, "meaningful to me" should not be excluded to activities where there is no compensation. I rejoice in the opportunity to engage in enterprises that bring value to others, meaning to me, not to mention a paycheck.

In his song "Real Life," John Mellencamp very nearly predicted the future reexamination of an aimless middle age and a workless retirement when he sang, "I want to live the real life, I want to live my life close to the bone. Just because I'm middle-aged, that don't mean I want to sit around my house and watch TV."

As we witness the great demographically driven expansion of the stage we call middle age, this is becoming an anthem of retirees. We clearly don't want to sit around and watch our midsections expand as our middle years extend. The trend of people choosing to work into their 60s, 70s, and even 80s is now a fact of life. Whether people choose to work for economic reasons, existential reasons, or an amalgam of the two, it is indisputable that the trend toward working longer is part and parcel of the retirement discussion. Whether we want to or have to, we can no longer separate work from retirement—and that's good news for all of us.

Research from Rand in 2009 pointed to the fact that people are choosing to work in retirement, and recent indicators point only to an increase in this trend.

Rand's research demonstrated that:

- Forty-four percent of retirees worked for pay at some point after retirement.
- Eighty-three percent of Baby Boomers intend to keep working after retirement.
- Fourteen percent of those currently working say they'll never retire.

A more recent study by the Insured Retirement Institute underscores this shift: 35 percent of Boomer-aged adults expect to retire after age 66, and 23 percent expect to work well into their 70s.[3]

People in their first stages of retirement describe *preference shocks*—where many individuals found retirement less satisfying than anticipated. Surprisingly, the study found that unfulfilled work expectations were much more common than unfulfilled leisure expectations. We also see that more and more people with a whole lot more unstructured time on their hands come to the realization that work has benefits, *many of which are nonmaterial.*

The bottom line is that the retirement pitch for the last generation has headlined the benefits of leisure, but those who enter into it full time are finding that leisure alone cannot deliver the life satisfaction they seek. The exclusively leisure-life retirement is a mirage, a message I have been broadcasting for the last decade. Individuals migrating from full-time contributors to full-time consumers cannot help but feel the existential shock to their systems. Self-indulgence is a poor prescription for a satisfying life. When some self-indulgence is balanced by service, relationship building, and exercise of aptitudes, it becomes a completely different story—with a much happier ending.

For good reason, over the past several years we've primarily been focused on the financial challenges surrounding retirement. What we hear far less about are the nonfinancial retirement challenges that people have been experiencing:

- *Sense of identity loss.* You were Dr. Jones for 40 years. Who are you now?
- *Social/Relationship challenges.* What if you actually enjoyed the people you were working with or calling on?
- *Change/Reduction in mental stimulation.* Can sudoku really fill the bill?
- *Psychological issues around not getting a paycheck.* Inflation can quickly make you paranoid about going to a movie.
- *Extra time to fill in the day.* Are you wandering in the garage for something to break so you have something to fix?
- *Anxiety/Depression.* She doesn't seem too thrilled to have you around 24/7, does she?

These are the real, existential risks of retirement that we must wrestle with. Add to this list concerns about money, inflation, and uncertainty in our markets, and it is no wonder that more and more people are coming to the same conclusion—it works to work. And that doesn't necessarily mean full-time work, but enough to meet your emotional, social, and intellectual stimulation needs. The New Retirementality will be different for every individual. You may want to devote 10 hours a week to volunteerism, whereas someone else may never slow their 40- to 50-hour workweek until they completely expire—for the simple reason that *their work energizes them.* The critical conclusion that you should draw from this discussion is that work should always be a part of your life because it provides more than a paycheck.

Financial needs are only one piece in this puzzle when it comes to the New Retirementality. In a Financial Research Corporation (FRC) study, the top four reasons people gave for continuing to work were:

1. Staying healthy (90 percent)
2. Money for extras (87 percent)
3. Staying socially active (82 percent)
4. The challenge (79 percent)[4]

All the money in the world won't make a difference for those who feel they are losing their health, their connectivity, and their sharpness due to the lack of real challenge. Clearly, being challenged and active are now being mined not only for longevity purposes but for quality of existence as well.

The Rand study stated, "The prevalence of un-retirement, as well as partial retirement, underscores the rising importance of multistage retirement transitions, not only as the outcome of uncertain realizations of the budget constraint after retirement, but also possibly through dynamic preferences for leisure."

Pay attention to the word *multistage*—this translates to each of us taking two to four attempts to achieve the balance and fulfillment we seek at the many different levels in life. It is not a one-and-done decision, as all of us require time and experimentation to find the proper balance between vocation and vacation in our lives. One of the reasons for this is that as we mature, work can take on an entirely different meaning in our life. It can become about more than producing a paycheck and paying the bills. As we have already discussed, many people simply *need* to work—and not just for money. Let's take a look at some familiar stages of work and then discuss the destination many of us are aiming at and hoping for.

Exploration Mode (Often Experienced in Our 20s)

This is where you "try on" careers to see how they fit. Early on, it is a process of discovering what you don't like doing more than anything else. Even within a particular discipline, for example, engineering, retail, or sales—you need to explore the various tasks within that discipline to determine which engagements are good fits for your personality, interests, and skill sets.

Utilitarian Mode (Often Experienced in our 30s and Onward)

This is working to meet obligations, make ends meet, and support a lifestyle outside of work. Many of us who segue from the exploration mode into the utilitarian mode simply have bills to pay and need a job that pays those bills. We may shift into this mode when we feel we have exhausted much of our exploration years and opportunities—we settle for the best option we have found in terms of work we find challenging and/or intriguing and pay we find acceptable.

Renaissance Mode (Often Experienced in Our 40s through Our 60s)

This is where we conduct in-depth examinations into our working lives. We identify the tasks and challenges that infuse us with energy and passion. We look for opportunities to capitalize as much as possible on our intellectual capital, relationships developed, and skills acquired, as well as personal interests and makeup. In this mode, we seek work that is affirming to us as individuals and provides deeper personal satisfaction.

Mission Mode (Can Be Experienced at Any Age but Takes Experimentation and Experience to Affirm)

This mode of work is driven by a sense of purpose that can be very general or specific. For instance, a general goal may be to help people learn, while a specific goal may be to help young people improve their math skills. Mission mode has as many forms of articulation as there are people. Those in mission mode work toward utilizing their time to fulfill a specific purpose that they view with a high degree of passion. When we are in mission mode, we rarely see ourselves as "having a job" or "going to work." These are the people who say, "I can't believe I get paid to do this!"

I am constantly on the lookout for people in mission mode because I'm keen on discovering what drives them. I was flying home from a presentation in Florida and had begun writing down thoughts about the place of work in our lives, specifically how we mature in regard to our work. I was coming to the conclusion that there are four "modes" of work that we can pass through in our search for meaningful engagement—the modes listed earlier. With the thought of *mission mode* in my head, I got up and walked to the galley area of the plane to see if I could get a soda. I began chatting with Frank, the lead attendant on the flight. I asked him how the merger was going with his recently acquired airline. He responded by saying that there were definitely bumps in the road but that it didn't have a whole lot of effect on his working life because he "brought a certain attitude to work each day."

"And what attitude is that?" I inquired.

"My work is my calling. It is my mission. I am here for you, the passenger, to make this the absolute best experience you can have. I am very blessed in my career. I see the world and get paid for it. I love seeing new places and all the perks that come with this career."

I told Frank that I was writing on that very topic at this moment and asked his permission to quote him. I was grateful for the instantaneous affirmation that we can evolve and mature through our work. We can eventually come to a place where our minds, our spirits, and our effusion of effort reach total assimilation.

One group at the leading edge of this discussion is Civic Ventures, founded by Mark Freedman of San Francisco. Go to their web site, Encore.org, and you'll soon see how they promote the idea of combining purpose, passion, and a paycheck (what I call "collecting a *playcheck*"). Encore.org will help you *learn* by finding out more about purpose-filled careers in the second half of life; *work* by starting your journey to a meaningful encore career; and, finally, *connect* by meeting the people and organizations making encore careers a reality. The establishment of the organization's "Purpose Prize" awards people over 60 who are "changing the world." The reward is much more than the $100,000 each award-winner receives—it's demonstrating that meaningful engagement is essential regardless of your age.

Mark Freedman makes the compelling case that the longevity revolution—pushing life expectancies closer to 100—are not adding to the end of our lives as much as they are adding to the "late middle" of our lives. Freedman says that a new stage of life is emerging, the working retired, as millions of Americans, who find themselves in a state of "suspended identity," are "un-retiring." Midlife is expanding like never before and is pregnant with possibilities for fulfillment for all of us. Work is a central theme in the discussion of this expansion. We can all benefit by answering the question, "What benefits of work mean the most to my well-being?"

Individual Retirement Attitude

I will engage in a thorough examination of what work means to my personal bearing, my loved ones, my sense of meaning in life, those I work with, and the things I work on. I will no longer blindly follow old assumptions about age and meaningful work engagements. I understand that meaning is a highly personal concept that may have significance to me but not others.

The Real Meaning of Work

An artist was asked what his favorite work was. He thought for a minute or two and then replied, "The next one."

I met Nils on a westward flight and, guessing he was close to retirement age, asked if he was retired. He said, "No. I tried that; didn't work so well." When I asked him to explain, he told me that he had left his job as a representative of a manufacturing firm and within weeks was stir crazy, wandering around the garage "looking for something to break so I'd have something to fix." Six months into retirement, his old firm called to see if he would be willing mentor some of the new guys and consult on some former accounts.

Nils had an epiphany on his first trip back to visit a former client: "They all jumped out of their chairs to greet me, wanted to catch up, and invited me to have a beer and dinner that night." The president of that particular firm asked Nils to come back to his office because he wanted to get his opinion on an issue they were facing. "They missed me," Nils said. "And at that moment, I realized that, in fully retiring, I had left all those meaningful social connections behind as well as my opportunities for solving problems, something I really enjoy." These people made Nils feel valued, useful, and productive—something we must all consider before we leave such connections behind in the wake of RV fumes.

We are long past the time where retirement was a "work or play" ultimatum. Any observer of the "reengagement in work trend" among the 65+ crowd can see and hear that this is about more than just paychecks, although paychecks certainly have their place. I have interviewed and heard stories from hundreds of people in this demographic group and can tell you that the benefits they seek are more noetic than material, but they always add, "The extra money never hurts."

A fundamental discussion with any potential retiree must include a discussion of the benefits of being at work regardless of age. With millions of retirees reentering the workplace within a short time of their retirement, it is no longer plausible to exclude this work discussion from the retirement discussion. Retirement is no longer an event—it is a segue into an altered definition of life as we know it.

Before anyone gets upset and feels as if I'm protesting against the leisure life they've worked so hard to achieve, let me clarify that when I use the term *work* in this discussion, I am not inferring rote and boring tasks, soulless endeavors, or daily drudgery. I am speaking about engagements that fit the definition of work I offered in the previous chapter: *an engagement that brings value to others and meaning to me.* Some retirees have approached me after a speech, indignant that I would speak any sentiment challenging the laid-back existence. One lady could barely contain her dislike of the idea, huffing, "Work! I've had enough." And I am sure she had. The problem is that she most likely had the work of drudgery. She had experienced the type of work that drained and exhausted her spirit—the ilk of career engagement that makes *work* a four-letter word for many.

In the chart in Figure 7.1 from the 2011 Retirement Confidence Survey, we see that people who go back to work are motivated by more than money in their decision to reengage the workplace. Half of the reasons cited—including the top two—are focused on psychological and existential payoffs: (1) staying active and (2) enjoying working. This study splits potential answers equally between economic and lifestyle benefits, so respondents are weighing in on both issues. Having benefits is a motivator to a little less than half of the respondents and money for extras was a factor to three-quarters of those surveyed. Money is involved, but just as important—and in some cases, more important—growth and health concerns are involved in the decision to extend one's work life.[1]

We'll dive deeper into money dynamics in Chapter 12, but for now we'll focus on the psychological, intellectual, and social factors that beckon us to forgo lives of total leisure and slow-moving calendars.

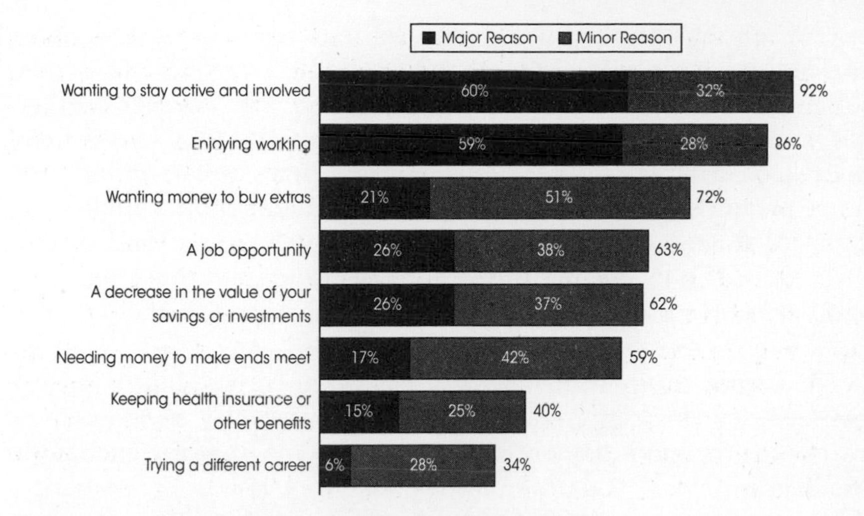

Figure 7.1 2011 Retirement Confidence Survey
Source: Employee Benefit Research Institute and Matthew Greenwald & Associates, Inc. 1993–2011 Retirement Confidence Surveys.

Brain at Work

We need to begin thinking in more holistic terms. What exactly do you want to retire from? Remember that the word *retire* means to withdraw, and I will grant that there may be aspects of our lives that we may need to withdraw from to varying degrees. If there are aspects of work inducing more stress than satisfaction, such as a highly bureaucratic environment, wearying commute, or disingenuous supervisors, some withdrawal may be prescribed.

Think of withdrawal in a compartmental sense and your opinion of withdrawing completely from the workplace will probably be transformed. You may want to withdraw from the environment you are in, but do you want to withdraw from taking on problems and solving them? You may want to withdraw from a monomaniacal boss, but do you want to withdraw from the meaningful connections you make in your work? You may want to withdraw from a grinding commute, but do you want to withdraw your intellect from the creative stimulation it receives when you develop solutions to complex problems?

Alzheimer's and dementia research is underscoring the power of leading an intellectually challenging life, *especially as we age.* Research suggests that stimulating the mind with mental exercise may cause brain cells, called neurons, to branch wildly. The branching causes synapses (connections between brain cells), adding millions of additional connections as we challenge our intellectual capacity. Arnold Scheibel, a professor of neurobiology and former director of the UCLA Brain Research Institute, says that we should think of our brain as a computer with a bigger memory board: "You can do more things more quickly."

A recent study from French researchers has found a link between delaying retirement and reducing one's risk of Alzheimer's and other forms of dementia. The study found that for each additional year of work you put in, you reduce your risk by 3.2 percent.[2]

Ironically, one of our greatest fears around aging is that our brains will do less at a more sluggish pace. We must treat the brain like the highly sophisticated muscle it is and not allow atrophy to set in because of a lifestyle that taxes it too little. Deficient intellectual challenge equals slowed synapse development and opens the door to degenerative conditions.

New knowledge about the brain began emerging from a small convent in Mankato, Minnesota, almost 20 years ago and has been affirmed in recent years. The study started with the School Sisters of Notre Dame, where longevity was the rule. The nuns lived to an average age well beyond the norm. Almost a quarter of those residing there lived well beyond 90. Not only did they live longer but also they didn't experience dementia, Alzheimer's, or other brain issues nearly as often as the general population. The nuns have been studied for years by the Sanders Brown Center on Aging at the University of Kentucky. The Center concluded that those nuns who earned college degrees, taught, and constantly challenged their minds lived longer than those who engaged only in physical activity.

Any engagement that we find intellectually stimulating serves as a stimulus toward dendritic growth, which is the equivalent of expanding the computing capacity of our brains. Brain researchers encourage us to search out areas that are diversions and unfamiliar to us, intellectual pursuits that feel challenging. These pursuits become the fulcrum for dendrite expansion in our gray matter. The research indicates that it is never too late. If we treat life as a learning experience and are intentional about continued learning, we are constantly building and expanding our brain circuitry.

Invest in Who You Are

"Strive not to be a success, but to be of value."

—Albert Einstein

The discussion surrounding "who we are" has received short shrift in the retirement conversation and has resulted in many *About Schmidt*–type retirements. For those who haven't seen the movie, Jack Nicholson plays a 60-something retiree going through the existential crisis of no longer knowing who he is or why he matters. Personally, I found it to be more terrifying than *The Shining*. Most men are unprepared for the realities that come crashing down around them: their golf game isn't getting better, their family doesn't want them visiting *that* much, their wives need space, and they don't know where to ply a lifetime of know-how and know-who any longer.

I ran into my attorney, Dan, on the eve of his 60th birthday. It was later in the evening and he had been celebrating the occasion with a group of friends. I offered birthday greetings and asked what it was like turning 60. He said, "In one way, it's terrible. When you turn 60, everyone feels obliged to ask you, 'When are you going to retire?' I've thought long and hard about this, and one thing I know for sure—I *love* solving people's problems. I get to work with bright and successful people and do important work for them. I want to go out the way our founding partner went out—he fell dead in his 80s coming back from lunch while still working on a case."

Dan went on to tell me of one of the more colorful approaches to nonretirement I've ever heard of: "I've watched retired neighbors over the years work out in their yard, mowing, trimming, shoveling, and I know this about myself—it's not for me! My neighbors thought I'd gone loony, but I packed up every garden and lawn utensil I owned and put them all on the curb for the garbage collectors to take away. Now I know I have to stay at work to be able to pay the service that does all that work for me!"

The old retirement question was "How will we invest your money so you can retire comfortably?" The New Retirement question is "How will you invest yourself and your time, as well as your money?" One method I have created for getting at the investment of "who we are" is to guide people in a conversation around *working benefits*—what we derive from our work that is worth keeping in motion on at least a part-time basis.

Working Benefits

WORKING BENEFITS—Below the surface of working for a paycheck lies the question, "Why do you work?" Look at the following list of qualitative work benefits and ask yourself how important each aspect is to you (1 is least important; 5 is most important).

Physical health/Energy	1 2 3 4 5
Intellectual stimulation	1 2 3 4 5
Social stimulation	1 2 3 4 5
Creative tasks	1 2 3 4 5
Competition	1 2 3 4 5
Meaningful contribution	1 2 3 4 5
Sense of relevance	1 2 3 4 5
Solving problems	1 2 3 4 5
Engagement/Doing what you love	1 2 3 4 5
Opportunity for growth	1 2 3 4 5

Individuals who are wise enough to avoid jumping off the work cliff and instead have decided to negotiate the type of balance and application that best suits their lives are reaping the benefits today. I have had the privilege of hearing many such stories firsthand. Here are a few that might provide some insight and inspiration to you as well:

- David Leo, acting on a lifetime of gathered knowledge and industry understanding, is coaching financial professionals at 75 and has no immediate plans to ever completely quit. His experience and wisdom are valuable to others, and it is meaningful to him to share these gifts with others. I had the pleasure of having dinner with David in New York City and was impressed with his curiosity, his keen eye for solving problems, and his desire to grow when a lot of people are sitting around talking about the good old days.
- Upon her alleged "retirement" from serving as a quality control inspector for a chain of southeastern gas stations—which called on her to use her camera a lot—Sondra Ettlinger converted her interest in photography into a series of lectures and got herself and her husband a gig traveling the world, basically

for free, by giving entertaining lectures on cruise ships about making the best use of one's travel photos. Eventually, she switched to lecturing about genealogy, another interest of hers. These days, she mostly lectures about the ports of destination. She's hitting her upper 70s and still travels all over the world several times a year. If you want to take a peek, visit her web site at www.ettlingerproductions.com.

This story was sent to me by her daughter, Wendy, who says she gets worn out just thinking about her mother's schedule these days. She also wrote, "This book also has been a great boon in my life, too. It was one of the factors that helped me leave corporate America, move out to Oregon, and establish my own successful business five years ago. Not ready to call it retirement yet, but living the good life, for sure!"

- Gregg from South Africa sent me this invigorating anecdote about some retirementors that he knows: "I consulted with a client a few years ago who at 87 was still working as a doctor—because he wanted to—mostly doing volunteer work at a local government hospital . . . he came in with his son who was desperate for him to retire but his response was 'Why, what would I do all day long?' He had also recently completed some further studies that allowed him to continue working. I also have a client who retired as head master of a local school and has gone back to work at a private school as their headmaster—partly for the income but mostly because he was afraid of doing nothing all day long."

There are plenty more stories because the majority of the emerging generation has rejected the latent, leisure-focused, and particularly passive lifestyle that previously characterized retirement living. There is still more life to squeeze out from living, and for many of us, being at work has something to do with it.

Collecting a Playcheck

"Do something you love and you'll never have to work a day in your life."

—George Burns

What you spend your life doing should be fulfilling to you—period. If it's not, you need to take responsibility and commit to making a change. How do you go from collecting a paycheck to collecting a playcheck? Life is simply too short to settle for a lukewarm existence. If you're not spending your time doing something fulfilling, it's time for a career assessment and transformation. If you are looking toward retiring, you'll want to address the need for the expression of work, to some degree, in your life ahead. Most people don't conduct a work assessment before retiring but end up taking on part-time work within a short period because they realized they were missing out on positive aspects of work.

In this exercise, you have the opportunity to compare your working situation against the seven factors of fulfillment at work:

1. How well your talents and abilities are utilized.
2. Your enthusiasm level toward your work.
3. How much fulfillment you derive from the work you do.
4. The quality of the people you work with.
5. The growth you experience as a result of your work.
6. The benefit to others that is created through your work.
7. The degree that you are energized by what you do.

You collect a playcheck when you have so much satisfaction doing what you're doing that you can't believe someone is paying you to do it. With introspection, guidance, and persistence, you can find work that will reward you with a playcheck.

Directions: On a scale from 1 to 5, rate yourself on your true level of contentment, (with 1 being "not content" and 5 being "completely content").

1. I feel as though my natural talents and abilities are expressed through my work.	1	2	3	4	5
2. I have a continuing enthusiasm about the work I do.	1	2	3	4	5
3. I often feel energized by the work I do.	1	2	3	4	5
4. I enjoy the people I work with.	1	2	3	4	5
5. My work helps me to grow intellectually and personally.	1	2	3	4	5
6. I feel that I bring benefit to others through my work.	1	2	3	4	5
7. I have a sense of serenity regarding my work.	1	2	3	4	5

Directions: Now that you've rated yourself, jot down what you like best and least about your job.

What I like best . . .	What I like least . . .
1.________________	1. ________________
2.________________	2. ________________
3.________________	3. ________________
4.________________	4. ________________
5.________________	5. ________________

What stands out to you after conducting this examination? Are you reaping little holistic benefit in your current working environment? If so, it might be time for a shift into another environment. Are you reaping benefits but want to slow down? In that case, working some balance into your schedule will sustain your enjoyment of the work you do. Are you reaping great benefit and enjoying a number of aspects of your work to this day? If so, full retirement probably is not going to suit you.

It is a healthy exercise to determine all the working benefits that you most appreciate. Money is an obvious benefit, and having more certainly doesn't hurt. But the examination doesn't stop with counting and cashing the check or the material benefits. The psychological, social, intellectual, and general well-being benefits that the proper application of work can deliver into your life is much more difficult to count or estimate in terms of the value it delivers to you and to those you work for. I'm confident that if you asked Nils, Sondra, Dan, or the 87-year-old doctor the question, "What is your favorite day of work?," they would answer, "The next one."

Individual Retirement Attitude

I am going to spend the necessary time to reflect on the transcendent aspects of work that infuse my inner being. I understand that, because I am unique, it will take specific (and possibly many) types of engagements to satisfy my working soul. I have much to give, and I will choose to contribute where I can bring the greatest value and absorb the greatest level of meaning.

Extending Your Stay by Staying on the Edge

"Thus, one way to resist aging is to keep working; by doing this mature workers combat invisibility and 'stay young' by 'staying active.'"

—Sargent, Lee, Martin, and Zikic, 2012[1]

My friend Scott told me of a sad but instructive tour he was once given of a floor at his former company (a Fortune 100 company) in New York City. It was called the "Dinosaur Floor" and was literally a way station for employees in their late 50s and early 60s, who were, at best, static contributors but most likely were regarded as "hangers-on." Many of the residents were former big players in the organization, but for one reason or another were now regarded as irrelevant. They knew the reputation of their morose destination and also understood that the corporation was no longer looking at any of them as primary contributors. Nonetheless, they were abiding in a state of stalemate as the corporation was most likely attempting to avoid age discrimination lawsuits.

Scott's observation was that a lot of the people who ended up there had lost their relevance because they failed to keep up with key changes in the organization. They had plenty of experience and were battle-tested but had stopped learning. They had lost the pulse of critical knowledge regarding what was going on in the company and who the generators of change were. Like dinosaurs, they were respected because of the size of their footprint, but also like dinosaurs, they became extinct because they refused to adapt to their changing surroundings. Scott said it had nothing to do with their work ethic or even age. It simply had to do with being current and by staying current. Scott told me he learned a valuable lesson that day, "The fact that you have 35 years in a company or industry means very little, if you don't stay current—there is no badge for experience." Relevance is the key to survival.

My attorney, still practicing full time in his late 60s, said he observed a similar pattern among partners who had become irrelevant. The first thing he noticed was that they no longer read the trade journals, which is key for keeping up with the changes and trends in the industry. That was the first step in losing touch with the pulse. My attorney called it the beginning phase of intellectual laziness.

Staying in Your Zone

After speaking in New York City, I met Phil, who told me that he had retired from the Army at age 52—everyone's dream back in the 1990s. He knew he was much too young to "act retired," so he went to work for a year and a half at a major insurance company. His thought at the time was that working in customer service and reaping a reasonable income would be good for him. Phil soon discovered that the job was a long-term project that he wasn't really interested in sustaining after the Army. He wanted a game plan that energized him and knew he needed to get himself into a more energetic "zone."

Phil opted to go to a private company that engaged in transactional sales, which fit his personality very well. He ended up working there for eight years—full time. He then went on to work for the Commonwealth of Pennsylvania while continuing to work part-time at his sales job for another six years. I met Phil when he was 72 (he looked not a day over 60), and he is now working full time for the Commonwealth, enjoying the challenge and with no plans for exiting any time soon. I asked him if he had any advice for those who wish to extend their careers into their late 60s and 70s and he offered the following observations:

1. Money matters. When I retired, my income dropped but my bills did not.
2. Sustainability matters. Trying to work at something that just "wasn't me" could not be sustained. Probably no job is perfect, but it has to be rewarding "enough."

3. Willingness to "bounce around" is a big advantage. It became obvious that knowing exactly what retirement would entail was not clear ahead of time—and I wasn't alone!
4. Older workers have a great "work ethic," which is apparent to employers who have used them before.
5. Older (retired) workers have a big "liability": if things get difficult, they can just quit. (I don't think employers know that yet, but I have experienced it as a supervisor!)
6. Younger workers have a lot to teach us.
7. Younger workers are quite interested in listening to and learning from older workers—if they (the older ones) respect them.
8. Being willing to take orders from a (competent) supervisor 40 years your junior better not be a problem.

Yes Sir, Kiddo

A 2010 CareerBuilder poll of 5,200 workers found that 69 percent of workers 55 or older have younger bosses. Aside from the implied challenges of reporting to someone the same age as your kid (or grandkid in some cases), there are communication preference challenges to be overcome as well. Technology changes have a lot to do with this possible chasm in connecting. The younger generation's view is that "the dinosaurs" need to figure out how to get along with their younger and smarter superiors. You'll be expected to learn to communicate at their technological level and to respect their ways of approaching the job. It's either humble oneself and learn to adapt or off to the bone-yard you go.

Claire Raines, coauthor of *Generations at Work: Managing the Clash of Veterans, Boomers, Xers, and Nexters in Your Workplace*, encourages the older worker to adapt to a younger boss's communication style rather than try to fight or change it.[2] Many mature workers can get easily agitated at the younger generation's mesmerized attention to electronic messages and avoidance of eye contact when communicating, but these days it's the norm, so you'll need to learn to deal with it.

A reader sent me an entertaining anecdote about an 87-year-old who taught a geography course at the University of Minnesota. He still utilized a 1970s-era slide projector in his class and refused to use a laptop. Being autonomous in one's profession affords one the luxury of resisting technology shifts, if desired, but the rest of the aging workforce will need to reset their attitude toward adapting and learning.

Jac Holzman is an example we would be better off emulating. Jac, a technophile from the start, started Electra records in his home in 1956; he eventually sold the company to Warner in 1970. In 2013, at the age of 81, having never lost his love of all things technology, he released an iPad app that chronicles the career of Jim Morrison and the Doors. When interviewed on why someone his age is dabbling in creating apps, Holzman quipped, "Wherever technology impacts music, I'm going to be there." We would do well to adapt a similar perspective on our particular field of interest and passion.

Raines advises that even when the older worker makes an effort to learn new modes of communication, they shouldn't expect reciprocity. You need to adopt your boss's habits. Don't expect him or her to learn yours. Robin Throckmorton, coauthor of *Bridging the Generation Gap: How to Get Radio Babies, Boomers, Gen Xers, and Gen Yers to Work Together and Achieve More,* encourages older workers to take the initiative and have a conversation with their boss about the boss's favored mode of communication.[3]

The parties researching this phenomenon do agree that older workers shouldn't assume that having more experience will win them any degree of respect from a younger supervisor. "You have to earn that respect" is the advice of Throckmorton.

According to the U.S. Census Bureau, the average age of the industrialized Western workforce has been steadily growing. By 2050, over one-fifth of the U.S. population will be 65 or older, up from the current figure of one-seventh. The number of centenarians worldwide will double by 2023 and double again by 2035.[4]

Business has not kept the pace in planning for work population aging, but delaying the inevitable isn't going to remain an option for much longer, according to an editorial in the *Harvard Business Review* by David Bloom and David Canning, economics professors at the Harvard School of Public Health, titled "How Companies Must Adapt for an Aging Workforce."[5]

Their opinion is that, even though unemployment is relatively high now, as labor markets tighten—especially in Europe and Japan—companies will soon have little choice but to welcome older employees. Smart businesses aren't waiting; they are already preparing to capture and encourage the contributions of older workers. The authors believe that this approach will soon be regarded as a key competitive advantage. They believe that most of today's businesses underestimate and are ill-prepared for how far this trend will expand: "In the near future, employees in significantly growing numbers will likely be able to work productively into their eighth or even ninth decade."

Bloom and Canning advise those who stay in the workforce to not expect their pay to automatically keep climbing all the way to the end of their careers. "Seniority-based pay sometimes exceeds performance at the latter stages of the life cycle," they write, but the effect will be that "bringing pay and performance (properly assessed) into closer conformity would likely ease corporate norms surrounding age at retirement." In other words, some younger worker may be getting more pay, but you're still getting the satisfaction of being employed and earning a paycheck.

Ageism on the Radar

Ageism lawsuits are on the rise and will most likely continue to escalate. According to the Equal Employment Opportunity Commission, charges of age discrimination reached 23,465 in fiscal year 2011. That figure represents a roughly 40 percent uptick since 2006, when the figure stood at 16,548.

Many of us will simply refuse to be categorized as unproductive simply because of age. There is a growing disdain among more mature workers regarding being shut off from mainstream workplaces. Often today, when a 60- or 70-something person hears terms like *senior citizen* or *golden-ager*, he hears them as euphemisms for "used up" or "useless." Today's employer will have to reassess hiring and retirement practices tainted with ageism. Gray hair and wrinkles are no reason to refuse admittance to or invite departure from a workforce if the gray matter is still intact and the desire is still present. We will be hearing more about age prejudice and ageism settlements in the next few years.

Societal and corporate laws and practices will have to change to accommodate updated definitions of *old* in our society. And have no doubt about it: the 60+ crowd will have the clout to get the job done. This is a generation that is defined by their abilities—not by their date of birth.

The Teaching Bridge

One method that many retirement-age workers are employing to keep their skills and minds sharp is to teach a course on their specific specialty in the marketplace or on a topic where they are expert. The design, development, and teaching of courses by mature adults for their peers has become common in the learning-in-retirement programs found on university and college campuses around the United States.[6]

These programs are built on the model of older adults' creating learning opportunities for themselves and their peers within their local communities. These programs rely almost exclusively on volunteer instructors to develop and teach an array of classes for their members. The course offerings are extensive, and the course scheduling quite often copies the traditional college semester format of fall, winter, and spring terms. Is there a course you could teach for a local college that they could offer to your peers? It might be worth looking into local offerings in the learning-in-retirement space. What you may find is that some of your peers are doing the same and others are filling the seats. Teaching others will keep your senses sharp and your curiosity keen as you explore for after-retirement opportunities.

There is also a growing group of semiretired instructors in the Experience Corps, which has more than 300 volunteers working at 20 inner-city schools and reaching out to students who can really benefit from their experience, and spending time in classrooms, helping children achieve their potential. The Experience Corp is a part of the AmeriCorps national service network. Every year, AmeriCorps supports the engagement of nearly 75,000 Americans in service to meet critical needs in education, the environment, public safety, homeland security, and other areas. Audrey Weems became a volunteer for seven years: "I see beautiful changes. They come in sometimes and they seem tight . . . and we have a tendency to help them to loosen up and be conducive for learning and helping themselves."

If you want to stay sharp, stay engaged—even if there is no pay involved at the time. To be marketable one must be active, passionate, and involved with meeting needs on some plane. "Down time" need not get you down if you raise your level of vision toward meeting needs that match up well with your competencies, interests, and drivers.

Advantages of Underemployment

A report from the Transamerica Center for Retirement Studies shows that, though retirement historically has represented unemployment, you are better off being underemployed as opposed to unemployed. Aside from earning additional income, there can be access to employer health coverage and the opportunity to delay withdrawals from retirement accounts. Typically, household savings is relatively low among displaced workers, but their nest eggs are triple those of the unemployed, ratifying the idea that it's better to be underemployed than unemployed.[7]

Catherine Collinson, the president of the study, says, "The number of unemployed who are not considering proactive approaches to improve their financial outlook is alarming and suggests that many feel overwhelmed or discouraged." She suggests that an axiomatic first step toward regaining confidence is to realign your skills with prospective employers' needs. Collinson believes that underemployment trumps employment simply because the underemployed tend to demonstrate a more proactive approach to their situation; are more flexible toward making work-related changes, like switching industries or professions; are more inclined to seek additional education; and are more amenable to making lifestyle changes. In short, they demonstrate more elasticity.

On a trip to speak in Florida, I was driven to my hotel by a Vietnamese immigrant who transported my imagination with his story of elasticity and resilience. He had been a "boat person," and his entire family escaped Vietnam in the 1970s on a boat so overcrowded that "if one person had leaned to the side, we would have all drowned—the water was up to the windows in the lower deck." It had cost his family their entire life savings to make the perilous voyage. He came to the United States in 1980 and studied engineering and went to work for a major corporation for the next 30 years. And then "they decide to downsize me." His options? Move to Germany and take work or stay in Florida and take bridge employment (in this case, driving a limo) and continue to look for work.

"I have a wife," he told me, "and she doesn't want to live in Germany. So I will do what I can until I can do what I want again. Family is more important to my life than the money right now." If engineering work did not surface, he would begin thinking of starting his own business. I had no doubt that his positive, industrious, and resourceful attitude was the product of all he had lived through. This was just one more voyage—he had already survived the most dangerous one he would ever face.

The process of "recareering," as it is called in a study by Richard W. Johnson, Janette Kawachi, and Eric K. Lewis of the Urban Institute (*Older Workers on the Move: Recareering in Later Life)* is quite common and will become even more common if Baby Boomers—who are fast reaching retirement age—follow through on their plans to work in retirement. A large force of workers indicates that they want to try something new before fully retiring. One aspect of the study I found interesting were the comparisons between old and new jobs: they illustrate the trade-offs between the material and the holistic aspects of employment. It might be because many of us choose to move in less demanding situations, but here are some of the findings:

- Hourly wages are substantially lower on new jobs than former jobs for all older career changers. Median wages fell by 57 percent for retirees, 22 percent for those who were laid off, and 5 percent for those who quit their former jobs.
- Nearly a quarter of career changers lose health insurance when they change jobs; only about 10 percent gain insurance.
- Older workers who change careers are most likely to move out of managerial jobs and most likely to move into sales or operator positions.
- Older career changers—especially those who have retired—are more likely to have flexible work schedules on their new jobs than on their old ones.
- Stressful working conditions fall sharply in the new jobs of older career changers.
- The large majority of older career changers say that they enjoy their jobs, but they are more likely to enjoy their new jobs than their old ones. This tends to be the case despite a decline in the prestige score, or social standing, of the new careers.[8]

EntreMature

Another interesting trend of our times is the number of traditionally retired-age individuals who are venturing into entrepreneurial pursuits. Eighteen percent of the entrepreneurs (people running their own business) surveyed by AARP describe themselves as "retired." In fact, the fastest-growing age group of entrepreneurs is over 55. The modern retirement seems to include working for more than a quarter of those surveyed. "These days, the difference between our regular working life and retirement may be more a state of mind," said Jean Setzman, vice president of financial security at AARP.[9]

Mature adults represent a growing share of new entrepreneurs, thanks to an aging population but also a rising rate of entrepreneurship among that group, according to the Kauffman Index of Entrepreneurial Activity. One in 10 people who work for someone else now said they plan to start their own business when they retire, according to the survey of about 1,500 adults aged 45 to 74. The survey also found that 15 percent of workers in that age group currently describe themselves as self-employed. Fully 30 percent of those self-employed workers said they started their own business after losing a job. And here's some good news: 72 percent of the self-employed workers surveyed said they turned a profit in 2011.[10]

In an article about entrepreneurship in older adults, Nancy Strojny, chairwoman of the Portland, Maine, chapter of SCORE, a nonprofit that offers free mentoring to aspiring business owners, states: "People should not buy the myth that all they need is a good idea. In reality, it's never the idea, it's always the execution." She would know, as she is also the owner of her own business, Beauty Vantage Consulting, a marketing firm focused on the hotel industry.[11]

The article went on to say that mature adults often have the unique skills required to start and succeed in business. Helen Dennis, coauthor of "Project Renewment: The First Retirement Model for Career Women," says that the more seasoned veterans of work "know how to get information, connect with people, ask good questions. They come with experience and wisdom, know-how, and focus."[12]

Finally, Andrea Coombes, author of the article, offers the following tips:

- *Take time to prepare.* Michele Markey says planning and research are the keys to succeeding. She is vice president with Kauffman FastTrac, a hands-on education program for entrepreneurs, sponsored by the Kauffman Foundation. "It doesn't guarantee success, but their chances of succeeding are greater." Her organization provides a self-assessment that shows how ready you are for the transition into entrepreneurship. This transition can't be taken lightly as the commitment of time and money can be quite significant. If you and your spouse are not on board, then transition may not go so well.

- *Get help.* Nancy Strojny of SCORE advises that you find someone who "will tell you the truth—not what you want to hear," said Strojny. People are "so in love with their idea" that they're often blind to the facts. SCORE offers mentors, but a former partner, peer, colleague, or long-time can also act as an advisor. You will want to consult with more than one person who has blazed the same trail to find out where the pitfalls are and what the price of commitment truly is to succeed.
- *Assess the investment required.* The most important question up front is, how much can you afford to lose? If you're going to tap your 401(k) and you don't have other reserves to fall back on, it may be necessary to get a partner or not to pursue the venture at all. Experts advise that you resist the urge to lock in big costs up front, like renting a plush office space right out of the gate. "Until you really test the water that this idea has legs or traction, you don't want to tie yourself into fixed costs," Strojny said.

  Those who have succeeded often looked for shared workspaces where they could rent a desk and office space. It is not only cheaper but can offer networking opportunities as well. "There are decisions that Boomers need to make that are unlike a 20-something," said Markey of the Kaufman Institute. Extra caution and prudence are required when the volume of earning years is behind you.
- *Consider a franchise.* "Franchising can be appealing to older entrepreneurs because the learning curve is shorter," Markey said. "A lot of the legwork has been completed. They're not having to reinvent the wheel," she said. The Entrepreneur's Source—which also happens to be a franchise business—offers free consultations to help people assess what type of franchise business might suit them. The company is paid a placement fee by the franchise if and when a person decides to buy in.
- *Bend but don't break.* After interviewing scores of people in their 60s and 70s who continue to sustain their place or continually reemerge in the workplace, the one thing I can point

to as a contributor toward relevance in the workplace is elasticity. You may have to stretch yourself, learn new things, try out arenas that are unfamiliar, and deal with some neophobic emotions now and then. It may require a childlike curiosity at times and an aged resiliency at others.

The stereotypically aging person is one who slowly but surely pulls in their periphery until they live within a rote bubble of repeated patterns and habits. The elastic persona and soul is just the opposite: constantly stretching, trying, examining, and experimenting to find what best suits him or her at this stage of life. This elasticity is attractive to others, motivating to you as an individual, and tends to push the periphery of possibilities outward instead of inward as you move further from your date of birth. To stay on the edge you must never retreat from the edge.[13]

Individual Retirement Attitude

If I hope to extend my shelf life, I understand that I will need to do everything in my power to keep a competitive edge. I will not succumb to entitlement thinking no matter how long I've been at it and will earn every opportunity I get in the future based on merit and through ingenuity and initiative.

A New Mind-set: Retire on Purpose

"Too many people die with their music still in them."
—Oliver Wendell Holmes

This chapter is all about attitude. As we enter the third stage of life, the attitude we choose will have the greatest bearing on our fate. We are entering the final stages of a retirement revolution. The difference between evolution and a revolution is that with evolution, a critical core of proactive people see the inevitable coming and decide to hasten the arrival date. Without question, for the past 15 to 20 years the institution of retirement has been morphing into something other than what we are familiar with. The idea has been evolving slowly toward something other than a playground agenda for senior citizens. The revolution taking place is that many are seeing this stage of life as just the opposite—*the most fertile period of life for meaningful pursuit.*

The population of experienced adults could be divided into a set of attitudes toward this particular phase of life:

- The "I'm done" crowd
- The "I have to" crowd
- The "I'm inspired" crowd

"I'm Done"

I can sympathize with those of you who have suffered through years of grinding work with little satisfaction or corporate environments rife with selfishness, sabotage, and subterfuge. You have had enough and just want to trade in your business suit for sandals or golf shoes. As detailed in earlier chapters, you may be in for some unexpected surprises regarding the vacuum left within dispensing yourself from any sort of meaningful contribution or the continued exercise of competencies. This attitude is based on the premise of "I've earned this"—and you have. The future is yours to mold; just make sure you're not the one that is molding.

"I Have To"

Those of you who have adopted this stance toward your circumstances have had your plans disrupted. Whether it was the disappointment of a time of unemployment, stock market losses, or recession period realities affecting your career, when you say, "I'm working because I have to," you are telling the truth. However, this truth need not be a grudging, wholly obligatory death march into aging employment. For every mature worker I meet who has adopted the obligatory attitude, I meet another with a grateful attitude, who says, "Hey, things didn't work out according to plan, but thankfully I'm still healthy enough to work and I'm earning an income. I've learned to see the best in these circumstances."

It is attitude that makes a life, not vice versa. More important than the circumstance we face is the disposition we choose toward that circumstance. In *The Doctor and the Soul,* Victor Frankl wrote that in life we have a position (how and where we came to be), a destiny (what has happened), and a disposition (how we choose to respond to our "how and where" and "what has happened"). It is the disposition, or the "position taken," that ultimately defines the individual's life, not what happens and why.

Ask a cynic why he is a cynic and he will tell you it is because of his position and destiny—what happened and why it happened. Cynics have chosen the worst possible disposition: to give up on the possibilities because their rose garden may have contained some weeds. The all-important point they miss is that their disposition has deepened their unwanted position and entrenched them in a destiny they loathe. Your attitude—your "position taken"—toward events is what defines you, not the events.

The resilient, the survivors, the joyful, and the grateful seem to share a disposition that I like to characterize as the view of the "opti-mystic." Opti-mystics have found a way to see through the disappointment and prevailing circumstances and act resourcefully. They find opportunity and silver linings in undesired circumstances in order to find a way to strengthen what remains. Optimists see through the impediments and the fog of unplanned scenarios and recognize that:

Yesterday is irreversible.

Tomorrow hinges on our attitude today.

"I'm Inspired"

This contingent has decided to "retire on purpose"—whether they have to work or want to work. If you are part of the "I'm inspired" crowd, you are pursuing meaningful work with a paycheck attached or perhaps getting compensated spiritually or emotionally. Your stories are the accounts the rest of us can draw upon for personal inspiration and guidance. As a retirementor, you are paving a path of hopefulness and fulfillment for those of us who have yet to encounter this phase. Your stories, along with others' individual retirement stories, will reshape this planet as people begin to realize the revolutionary retirement attitude that changes everything: *I can make a difference now like never before.*

Why now more than ever before? Because you have experiences that have informed me. Because you know what works and what doesn't. Because you have clarity around what energizes my soul and what enervates it. As a result of my work, I have been blessed over the past decade to meet many such retirementors—their stories, vision, resilience, resourcefulness, and buoyant attitudes never fail to inspire me.

My own father's attitude fits this description. As of this writing, he is approaching his 79th birthday and still works each morning on a project for which we share enthusiasm. He handles syndication of my radio feature, *The Daily Dose,* which is heard on close to 150 stations around the country. I created this 90-second "attitude adjustment" to counter the unending flow of rants and politically infused railing that seem to dominate the airwaves.

Dad spent almost 30 years as a sports journalist in radio and television before switching to a sales career that lasted another 20 years. Seventeen years ago I asked him if he would take on the syndication work for my program, and he's still pounding the phones every morning. The work is not for the faint of heart. He hears 100 "nos" for every "yes," but he persists through the drought periods, and we're always thrilled when a new market jumps on board. Because of his resilience and indefatigable work effort, hundreds of thousands of listeners get a dose of inspiration to start their day in small cities and towns across the nation. Every time someone writes me or stops me to tell me that they listen and appreciate the messages, I think of Dad's tireless efforts. He knows what these attitudinal arrows can mean to someone's day. He wouldn't tell you he's retired, because he's not. But he is semiretired on *purpose* and he is grateful to be engaged.

I'd like to propose the following four attitudes that I have witnessed time and again in the lives of those 65+ years old that have caused them to flourish instead of flounder. Take the New Retirementality challenge and attempt to integrate these four attitudes in your own life:

1. I'll keep meaningful pursuit at the core.
2. I'll challenge my mind, body, and spirit.
3. I'll refuse to be defined by age.
4. I'll keep an eye on my "attitude instrument."

Meaningful Pursuits: A Midlife Crisis Gone Horribly Right

> *"The distinct priorities and values of this generation, coupled with the unique circumstances of their era, will create a new model for retirement—one that places a premium on meaningful and fulfilling activity and engagement in the community and one that creates an enormous reservoir of talent, energy, and experience that the country can ill afford to ignore."*
>
> —Hart Study on Retirement

If we buy into the idea that we are to get and give the most we can from our lives, then retirement at any juncture has new meaning and possibilities. Every month it seems I meet new examples of the New Retirementality—those who treat their lives as an evolving exploration mission. They are not content to sit around and watch television or simply bide their time with random busyness.

Marie Ens had served as a missionary to orphaned children and abandoned grandparents in Cambodia for 38 years when her denomination "invited her to retire at age 66." She politely declined. I asked her about her reasoning and she told me that "you don't retire from a calling." Our family sponsors two of the children in her home, and it's easy to understand how Marie was unable to walk away from these precious charges.

When visiting Place of Rescue for the first time, one can easily be drawn into thinking that this is an idyllic home, a place filled with perfect children laughing and happy, smiling grannies with wide (almost toothless!) grins. But beneath the laughter and wide grins, Place of Rescue is a haven—an oasis in a world that can be hard, cold-hearted, and downright mean. The fact is that this is a place where you encounter children who have overcome abandonment, grandmothers who are alone after losing their grown children to AIDS, and entire families who live under the daily shadow of HIV/AIDS.

Marie is a retirementor to me as an inspirational example of the idea that you don't have to be rich to live a rich life, and that you can't impose a retirement age on a heart full of purpose and meaningful engagement.

On the other end of the financial spectrum, I found another inspiring example of a purposeful approach in Ron Cordes, cochairman of Genworth Financial Wealth Management. He is also cofounder of the Cordes Foundation, which he and his wife Marty created in 2006.

In an interview with *Fast Company*, Cordes stated, "I spent the first half of my life building businesses designed to be the best in the world; for the second half, I really want to support businesses that are the best *for* the world." Cordes was looking for a way to link his "passion with his portfolio," after a life-changing trip to Uganda. He visited a village full of widows who had lost their husbands in the 20-year civil war. He decided to fund a microfinance program there that has helped many of the widows launch successful ventures with which they can support their children. He tells the story of a woman coming up to him and saying, "'We appreciate it when [white people] come to try to save our children, but we need to be able to save our own children. Thank you for investing in us so we can do that.' I'll never forget that moment." Fast Company called it a "mid-life crisis gone horribly right."[1]

Ron told me that his epiphany in that moment was that "empowerment was more powerful than pity." He decided to capitalize on his skills and expertise as a financial manager and use them in a way that would create more opportunities like this around the globe, where deep and persistent needs exist. He's calling this venture ImpactAssets, and they are involved in many ventures including microfinance, Fair Trade, sustainable timber, and renewable energy in the developing world.

Talk about a retirementor! Ron is the model going forward for those who want to continue to collect the "benefits" of work. I have no doubt that his efforts not only are making a difference in many lives, but also that he is reaping many benefits as well, including meaningful contribution, solving problems, a deep sense of personal relevance, and inspiring engagement. These are the transcendent payoffs of work, and we can no longer afford to leave them out of our "retirement" discussions.

The math of the new retirementality includes calculating how to best deploy financial assets—if we have any to share or spare—and how to capitalize on all the assets of our persona and identity. This is our social and soul capital and is, in my opinion, the next great frontier for so-called "retirement planning": unifying the discussions of managing monetary and social assets. The discussions we have been having around retirement have brought us to this place, but they cannot take us from this place. It can no longer be simply a "retirement" discussion, but instead must become a new retirementality discussion that helps us all define our next act.

You don't have to go to Africa or Cambodia to live out your purpose, but it's always helpful to be open to the possibilities. You may find your purposeful engagement around the block, down the street, or anywhere there is a need that stirs your heart and suits your skills.

This purposeful approach is now being recognized by the group Encore.org, which gives out $100,000 awards to recipients of its annual Purpose Prize. In 2012, winners included people who:

- Represented low-income homeowners in foreclosure.
- Brought safe drinking water to villages in India.
- Helped female parolees make a successful transition with job training, housing, and legal services.

- Taught life skills to low-income adults and teens.
- Brought seniors and foster care kids together to enrich each others' lives.

If you would like to think through your own purpose and direction, I would encourage you to work through the *Retiring on Purpose* workbook at the end of this book. This profile will help you to set your own direction and define the engagements that will be meaningful to you as you enter the third and potentially most promising stage of life.

Challenge Your Body, Mind, and Spirit

> *"This is the true joy of life: the being used up for a purpose, recognized by yourself as a mighty one: being a force of nature instead of a feverish, selfish, little clot of ailments and grievances, complaining that the world will not devote itself to making you happy."*
>
> —George Bernard Shaw

Going forward, it will be more beneficial to choose a posture of proactive health rather than get caught up in the health care system. You need to decide that this will be a vigorous and involved stage of life as opposed to a withdrawing and "retiring" stage. You can make the preparations you feel are necessary (such as long-term-care insurance), but the greatest impact to your health will be rendered by the New Retirementality decisions we make for holistic well-being, such as:

- *Work out your heart on a regular basis by walking, jogging, or some other aerobic exercise.* One study showed that walking three times a week for two miles adds five years to your life expectancy; decreases depression, diabetes, and cancer rates; and helps you sleep better. Cardiovascular challenge replenishes oxygen into your cellular system and improves the function of both body and mind.
- *Engage in regular, light weightlifting.* Lifting holistically produces not just physical strength and resilience but attitudinal and internal strength as well.
- *Maintain physical intimacy.* The head actuarial at a leading insurance company told me of a conversation he had with a 75-year-old woman who was rated for a 20-year life insurance

policy by his company. Having never seen this happen before, he called the woman to ask for the secret to her great health. Her reply: "Frequent and frantic sex."

- *Schedule charitable and altruistic activity into every week.* Those who feel a sense of purpose live longer and better.
- *Don't join the "moan and groan" sorority or fraternity.* Of course, we will have joints that hurt or don't work as well as they did, but we don't have to linger on them. Pessimism leads to an expedited health decline.
- *Engage in work or activities that utilize your talents and challenge your brain.* "Continuing to work keeps the mind sharp and the body healthy, which aids in maintaining a positive attitude," says Dr. Russell Clark, a 103-year-old real estate developer.
- *Drink a little coffee to start your engine and a little red wine to wind it down.* You've seen the studies. Cheers!
- *Examine your soul each day with reading, prayer, meditation, and checking of motives in word and actions.* Forgive those who offend, and love those who don't deserve it. It has been said that "grace is getting what we don't deserve, and mercy is not getting what we do deserve."

Stay focused on healthy living and follow some of the great examples of active and vibrant 80- and 90-year-olds. Your health habits will have a major impact on both your quality of life and the quantity of income available for that life. Think of health habits as an investment—in yourself. Physical discipline leaks over into mental focus, and mental focus and perspicacity leak over into introspection and a meaningful examination of our lives. It is the body influencing the mind, which is influencing the spirit, and the cycle continues back through the mind now inspired and the body now energized.

Refuse to Be Defined by Age

"While one finds company in himself and his pursuits, he cannot feel old, no matter what his years may be."

—Amos Alcott

Mapmakers in medieval times faced a problem. They were given the job of charting the continent but were not exactly well traveled themselves. So when they came to a border they had not crossed, they drew fire-breathing dragons toward their own country's boundaries. These maps, when viewed by the common masses, caused people to believe that if they crossed the border, they would be consumed by these infernal beasts. Needless to say, travel and adventure was limited. Many people, when challenged to try new things, to go to new places, or to try doing things in a different way, simply refuse. When asked, "Why?" they simply respond, "I'm too old"—they've been looking at aging maps with dragons.

Lydia Bronte wrote *The Longevity Factor* over 20 years ago, but the conclusions sound prophetic and eerily familiar with what we are witnessing even more frequently today. In her observations of a long careers study, she wrote:

> What emerges from their life stories is a view of the long lifetime different from what we might expect: an affirmation of the increasing richness of experience over time, of a deeper sense of identity, of a greater self-confidence and creative potential that can grow rather than diminish with maturity. It is obvious that seen through the eyes of the study participants, chronological age markers (like 65), which have held so much power in the past, are really culturally created—a norm that was accurate only for a particular place and time.

Why is it that when we talk of the maturity of money, we think of it as a positive form of growth; but when we talk about the maturity of people, we think of it as a time of depreciation? Within a decade or so we will see multitudinous examples of a great harvest of accomplishment and contribution coming after the age of 65 and even 75. There are thousands of examples out there right now—we just need to take notice. We can all try new ventures; we can all stretch our limitations, our abilities, our contribution, our reach, and our grasp. Each of us has the ability to test our endurance a bit further. Without taking risks, we settle into a quicksand called "complacency."

> *"The only thing that has ever made me feel old is those few times where I allow myself to be predictable. Routine is death."*
>
> —Carlos Santana

How old is old? What exactly do we mean when we say someone is old? Are we referring to the person's years on the planet or the person's state of being? Or both? By old, do we mean that a person is in a state of decline? Is there a predictable age when this decline commences for all people? Is "old" a man-made border? And do the dragons of decline exist mostly in our mind? Henry Ford said that when a person stops learning, he is old, whether he is 29 or 65. As you will discover throughout this book, there isn't much we can do about aging, but there is an awful lot we can do about growing old. We hold "old" at bay by focusing on successful aging.

Satchel Paige was arguably the best pitcher to ever play professional baseball. It is estimated that he won over 800 games in his unparalleled career. Because of racial boundaries, he didn't get the opportunity to display his talents outside the Negro leagues until the color barrier was broken by Jackie Robinson. When Paige did get his chance to pitch in the major leagues, he was elected the American League Rookie of the Year at the age of 43! Think about this. There is a very short list of men who have possessed the endurance to pitch at age 43. Paige was the Rookie of the Year at that age! He pitched in the majors until he was in his early 50s and continued to pitch professionally until he was 63 years old. Paige understood a few things about longevity.

Because of preconceptions about age and ability, Paige always tried to keep his age a mystery. Whenever he was queried about his age, he would provide a memorable quip like, "How old would you be if you didn't know how old you were?" or "I never look back on Father Time—he might be gaining on me."

We have many high-profile examples of achievers in our culture who are not looking back on Father Time, including Warren Buffett, still a leader in investment acumen in his 80s, and actress Betty White, in her 90s and more popular now than when she was on *The Golden Girls* or *The Mary Tyler Moore Show*.

And you probably have some great examples of "ageless wonders" in your own community. Study their example, their lifestyle, and, most important, their attitude. When I question these ageless phenoms, they always mention attitude as a key to thriving, regardless of age. Just as the ages of 62 and 65 are "artificial finish lines" for retirement, so also are any other ages that people cite when saying "he (or she) is too old for that." People are actively skiing in their 80s, racing in their 90s, walking and swimming in their 100s. Some people are working into their 11th decade. Examples of people crashing through age barriers and jumping over physical limitation hurdles are ubiquitous. A while back, I received a video from a family that had four generations perform a synchronized water skiing exhibition in North Carolina: their ages were 5, 40, 62, and 92!

Enduring Attitudes

The attitude instrument in an airplane tells you how your wings are aligned with the horizon. When I ask people to define attitude, they often talk of a mood or feeling or perspective. Moods and perspectives are certainly impacted by our attitude but, fundamentally, attitude is nothing more than *choosing a direction and sticking to it.* If we enter any phase of life without keeping our eye on the attitude instrument, the winds of adversity will tilt us and we will lose our bearings—and, more important, not make a safe landing. Attitude is the premier setting in our lives, as all other functions are eventually dictated by it.

I have always had a keen interest in the mind-set and attitudes of those who thrive in later life and have sought out the life stories of such for the last 30 years. As a kid I read about Satchel Paige. Later, I read autobiographies of people like George Burns, Winston Churchill, Albert Schweitzer, and Linus Pauling. Being a writer, I especially loved the stories of Norman Vincent Peale, Studs Terkel, and Peter Drucker.

One salient characteristic that leaps from the biographies of the "enduring" is their ready wit and lively sense of humor—especially regarding themselves. That those exhibiting longevity seem to share a *self-deprecating approach to life* tells me that such an approach is crucial to reducing stress. The connection between stress and illness is well established. The connection between one's attitude and stress level is obvious. Many of those I have read about seemed to possess not only a lively sense of humor but also other survivor attitudes toward life's stressors. Most were *forward looking* and concerned about the future as well as the present. Most refused to succumb to society's limiting views of age-related behavior and activity. They were people who truly believed they could control their own destiny.

A MacArthur Foundation study on aging described how one ages successfully.[2] The study used the phrase "a sense of mastery" to describe how individuals must believe in their ability to influence events and control their outcomes to be positive and productive in their later years. They found that during a period of less than three years, those who increased their sense of mastery also increased their productivity. The opposite also held true—those whose sense of personal mastery decreased saw a significant reduction in their involvement in productive activities. What exactly is personal mastery? Self-reliance.

The person who takes a passive approach to life and lacks the ability to take action will experience a lack of productivity at any age. Typically, as people age, their belief in their abilities and their power to control their own destiny grows. However, this belief can, if allowed to do so, reach a point of diminishing returns. Experiments and experience have shown that if people are *willing to try new things* in their mature years, their self-reliance and effectiveness can flourish to all-time highs. Stories abound of people creating new boundaries in their life in their later years—those who are flying on airplanes who have never flown, those who are taking up new courses of study, and those who are dabbling in new ventures and careers at ages others would consider old. Take, for example, Florence, who started driving an 18-wheeler semi at the age of 83 to become the oldest "rookie" in the history of the truck-driving industry!

As more of us prepare to spend a large part of our lives in "retirement," our attitudes toward this stage of life are extremely optimistic; 64 percent of us say we are currently enjoying either "the best" or "good" times in our lives. When you put a magnifying glass on the everyday activities and interests of the so-called retirees, you begin to see why their enthusiasm and optimism flourishes. They are a dynamic and engaged group of people. They object to traditional labels given to their age group, such as *elderly*, *old*, or even *seniors*. They see themselves as experienced, wise, and seasoned.

The numbers in these categories indicate a graying population that is healthy, active, adventurous, and more prosperous than ever before. These numbers only promise to rise with the influx of Baby Boomers in the 65+ category between now and the year 2030. In the 1960s, there were 17 million Americans aged 65 and older. Today, there are approximately 37 million. By 2030 there will be 70 million aged 65 and older. That number will be somewhere between 20 and 25 percent of the entire population. Depending on the attitudes you dictate for your own life, you can be one of the stories that your community will be talking about someday—someone who just gets better with age and rejoices with each day's opportunities.

You clearly have not reached the end of the road yet. There is a lot of territory to cover, and it might be wise before embarking on your next 100,000 miles to get "re-tired." Some fresh tread will serve you well. Find out how in the next chapter.

Individual Retirement Attitude

While your peers may be contemplating retiring on the beach or on the golf course, you can tell them you are retiring "on purpose." Beaches and games are good for respite, but purpose is best for the soul. Set your heart toward making the absolute most of your time, abilities, wisdom, and passions.

CHAPTER 10

The New Meaning of Re-tired: Your Next 100,000 Miles

"Do not think of retiring until the world will be sorry to see you retire."

—Samuel Johnson

When you buy a new set of tires, most tire shops will tell you that they will rebalance those tires at no charge to help you get the optimum life from your purchase. How often do you take advantage of the offer? If you're like me, you probably tell yourself that you will stop in periodically to check the balance, but actually you don't reappear until one or more has been worn down or you're experiencing a wobbly ride, and you are now forced to make another purchase. The analogy here is that—simply by virtue of use—things tend to go out of balance. So it is with our lives.

We're focused on our journeys and busy with our busyness. We begin to notice that the ride doesn't seem as stable or smooth as it once did, and we find that we are, again, out of balance. We're working too much. We're not seeing the people we want to see. We're not enjoying the activities that restore and invigorate us. We don't have any time to sit still and reflect. The balancing act of life is a dynamic challenge requiring a dynamic solution (continual reassessment). There is no such thing as a one-and-done rebalance for our lives. The tread gets worn and our alignment shifts by virtue of motion.

Achieving balance in life is a matter of constant focus and vigilance. Any good thing taken beyond the bounds of balance is no longer a good thing. Life is full of illustrations, as seen in the following about stepping over the invisible lines of imbalance:

- Physical rest becomes laziness.
- Physical pleasure becomes licentiousness.
- Enjoyment of food becomes gluttony.
- Self-care becomes selfishness.
- Self-respect becomes conceit.
- Cautiousness becomes anxiety.
- Being positive becomes insensitive.
- Loving kindness becomes overprotection.
- Judgment becomes criticism.
- Conscientiousness becomes perfectionism.
- Quietness becomes noncommunication.
- The enjoyment of life becomes intemperance.
- Interest in possessions of others becomes covetousness.
- Ability to profit becomes avarice and greed.
- Generosity becomes wastefulness.

There is an invisible line that we come to and can cross in all areas of life, which marks the difference between balance and imbalance, discipline and mastery, and chaos and control. We must constantly address and regulate the individual compartments of our lives to keep any particular focus from spinning out of control. Once we identify where the lines are that we should not cross and then develop emotional and logical thought patterns to keep us from crossing those lines, we achieve what is commonly called maturity.

New Spin on Re-tiring

Now we come to the specific balance desired in the "retirement" proposition. We have already established that a life of total ease will not satisfy. Neither will a life of nose to the grindstone without any respite. But the challenge, especially as couples retire, is that balance is a highly idiosyncratic proposition. What constitutes balance to you may be perceived as boredom to someone else. What constitutes balance to one person may be perceived as "too much going on" to that person's partner in retirement. How we each define retirement is as unique as our fingerprints.

For years, observers, researchers, and authors have been trying to reframe the retirement discussion by changing the term from *retirement* to something else. The word *retire* means "to withdraw," and the Baby Boom generation's discomfort with the notion of withdrawal has fueled the search and discussion for well over a decade to update the term. I've read about re-firement, re-hirement, re-wirement, and a slough of replacement terms like *renewal, renaissance,* and more. The efforts have been in vain as the term *retirement* is firmly entrenched in the life-course lexicon of modern life, in spite of its morphing meaning and definition.

So given this nomenclatural fact of life, I'd like to share an idea that my friend and sometimes coauthor Scott West proposes—keep the word *retirement* but alter its meaning without replacing the term. Here's the altered approach: since retirement is no longer considered an ending point on the map but more of a launching point, instead of withdrawing we need to recalibrate. What we need before we embark on our journey is to "*re-tire*" our vehicle—we need new tread for the journey ahead. Instead of hitting the final rest stop of life, we are now looking ahead to our next 100,000 miles. To re-tire then, is to prepare for the altered state of life ahead of us.

Thanks, Scott, for the idea. Now let's get busy getting re-tired. The analogy seems to jibe with the concept of balance and the fact that, as people embark upon re-tirement lifestyles, there are four primary categories of focus—the four tires if you will: *Vacation, Vocation, Renewal,* and *Relationships.* The task ahead of you is to idiosyncratically design a plan for balance that suits your temperament, your goals, and your specific situation.

I recently gave the profile in Figure 10.1 to a retired couple in which the husband had been in the retirement phase much longer than his wife, and they were struggling with how to manage their new schedule together. She didn't have any desire for more work but found herself becoming restless within a few months' time. He has worked three hours every day for the duration of his retirement years. After filling out the profile, many of their questions and the root of their recent discomfort became apparent, as they could see how, as individuals, they had unique personalities and perspectives toward retirement living.

My Retirementality™ Profile

Directions: *Within each group, choose the phrase that best describes you, with 4 being the best and 1 being the least. Total each letter on the bottom of the page. Do not leave any spaces blank, and be sure each group has a 1, 2, 3 and 4 rating.*

SAMPLE
A **3**
B **1**
C **4**
D **2**

A___I love to kick back and relax.
B___I love to spend time with family and friends.
C___I love exercising.
D___I love my work.

A___I want to spend more time on hobbies and other interests.
B___I want time to travel.
C___I want to exercise more.
D___I want to continue to do the work I do.

A___I want to get away from work.
B___I want to spend more time with my spouse.
C___I want to expand my interests.
D___I want to continue doing what I do for the rest of my life.

A___I want to visit a lot of places.
B___I want to catch up with a lot of friends.
C___I want to make staying healthy a priority.
D___I want to continue competing and finding new challenges.

A___I look forward to "every day is Saturday."
B___I look forward to spending more time with the people who are important to me.
C___I look forward to more personal growth.
D___I look forward to interacting with people I work with.

A___I want to play every day.
B___I want to plan some family trips.
C___I want to pay more attention to my well-being.
D___I want to use my abilities to help others.

A___I want to start working on my "bucket list."
B___I want to start making memories.
C___I want to focus on being in top shape.
D___I want to make a difference in the world.

A___I want to wake up to an empty agenda.
B___I want to be more involved in the community.
C___I want to increase my energy level.
D___I want to feel challenged on a daily basis.

A___I have many interests that take up my time.
B___I look forward to spending time with friends.
C___I want to lower my stress level.
D___I want to continue being able to use my skills.

A___Free time is my top priority.
B___I want to invest in relationships.
C___I want to find some balance.
D___I am completely engaged in what I do professionally.

Add up totals for each and record in the box below.

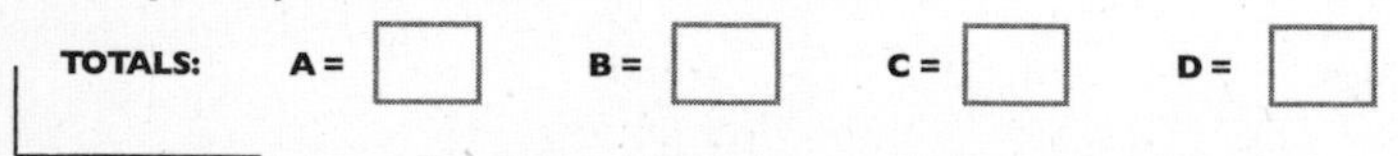

Figure 10.1 My Retirementality™ Profile

My Retirementality™ Profile

Directions: *Once you've totaled your findings, graph your "A" total on the Play line, "B" total on the Connect line, "C" total on the Renew line, and "D" total on the Work line. Draw a line to connect the dots. The results will help you and your advisor determine what is important to you and how to integrate your profile into your plans for the future.*

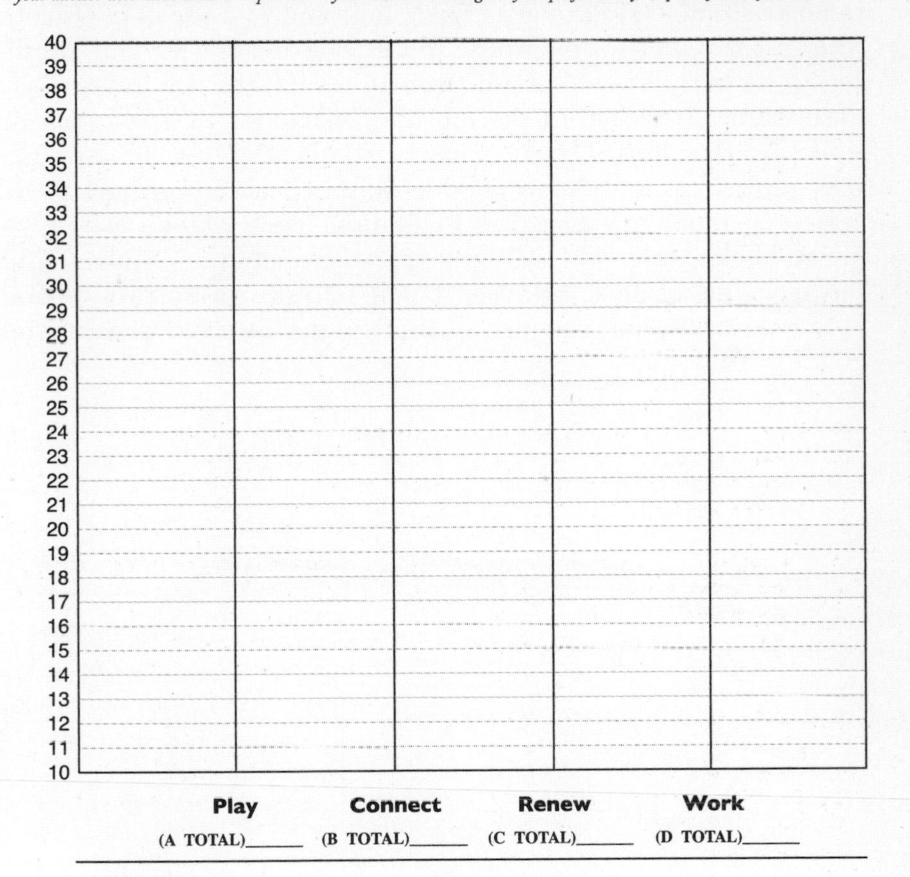

LEGEND

A. PLAY = LEISURE, TRAVEL, HOBBIES

B. CONNECT = TIME FOR FAMILY/FRIENDS

C. RENEW = PHYSICAL/MENTAL WELL-BEING

D. WORK = PROFESSION, HELPING OTHERS

Figure 10.1 (Continued)

Play

If you look at the simple chart in Figure 10.2 and first fill it in with your play activities, including leisure time, hobbies you'd like to engage in, and travel you'd like to pursue, you might reach some quick realizations regarding available time and your use of it. Usually, when I encounter people whose retirement dream is to "have nothing to do but play golf," I ask them to fill in their tee times. They enthusiastically block out the morning spaces on all seven days or sometimes five days. They now have 70 percent of their time staring back at them as white space. Suddenly, they realize they have made zero preparation toward activity to fill those blocks of time.

A weekly calendar will not represent all the ventures and engagements of an entire year, but it will give you a pretty good clue concerning the cadence of life you are directed toward. You

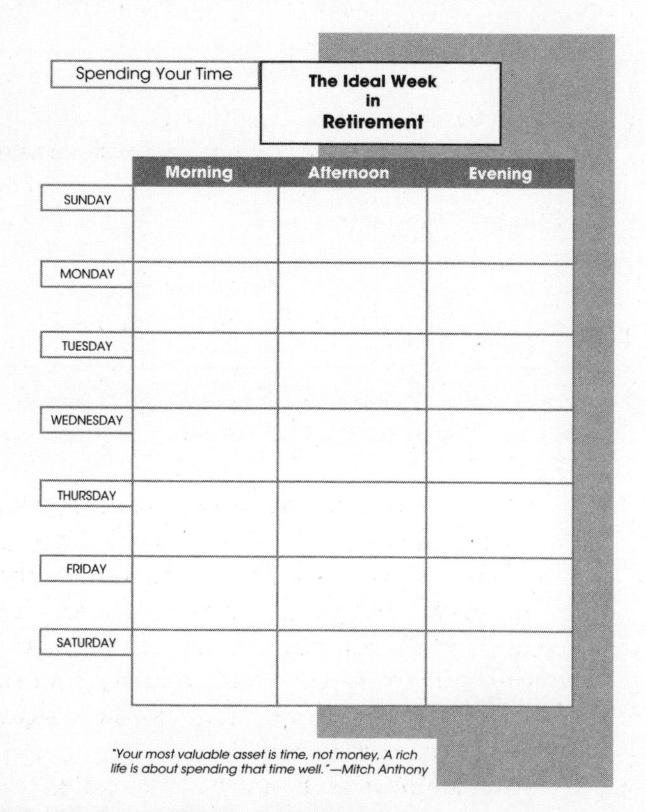

Figure 10.2 My Ideal Week in Retirement

probably won't be going on a trip every week, but you most likely will engage in hobbies and leisure several times in a seven-day period. Go ahead and fill in your calendar with work, play, connecting, and renewing activities and ask yourself, "What is the best use of my time during each day?"

Work

Keep in mind that work is no longer an either/or proposition when it comes to retirement; it is more of a *how much* proposition. How much do you need or want to work? How much do you enjoy the engagements that work brings to your mind and spirit? Gauging your capacity for work in your 60s to 90s is a highly idiosyncratic exercise—no other human can answer for you or know what work does or does not mean to you as an individual. The correct balance of work for you is determined by a number of factors including, but not limited to:

- How easily you are bored.
- How much you like your work.
- The potential strain on a marriage as the result of your being home all the time.
- Your need for additional income.
- Your energy level.
- The importance of your social network at work.
- Your need for competition.
- Your need for relevance.
- Your level of motivation and drive.
- Your need to create and make an impact.

The other factor to keep in mind while analyzing your retirement personality is that all of these factors (work, play, connect, and renew) are dynamic in nature and can fluctuate from year to year, depending on the circumstances you face. You may be heavily inclined toward play or work but if an unforeseen event like illness or injury takes place, your focus may steer toward connecting and personal renewal and then revert back again to your original focus once that particular period has passed.

Our lives are as unpredictable as are our responses toward circumstances we have yet to face or navigate through. Think of this profile as a measure of your DNA regarding the retirement lifestyle and as a compass for how you will navigate in the years ahead. No decision is permanent as long as there is potential for unexpected opportunities and temporary setbacks.

Connect

How much time you spend in connecting activities will vary with the geographical spacing of you and those you hope to connect with. If your children and grandchildren are in close proximity, then your schedule will most likely reflect that focus in your retirement profile. If your grandchildren are 3,000 miles (and a full day of travel) away like mine are, then the connecting calendar will be more annual, semiannual, or holiday driven. One chief consideration for those who place a high premium on connecting with others in their retirement vision is: *how much connecting does the other party seek?*

I'll never forget the scene in the movie, *About Schmidt*, where Schmidt, a retired insurance underwriter played by Jack Nicholson, is forced to face reality regarding his illusions of connecting grandeur with his daughter in a neighboring state. He had held the idea dear and set out from Omaha to Denver in his RV to see her. The scene is a couple of days into his long-imagined visit where he is sitting in a hot tub with a woman (Kathy Bates) and his daughter, and she asks him how long he plans on staying around. The disinviting tone is impossible to miss. The next morning he turns his RV back toward Omaha.

On a more inspiring note, I was once approached after a speech in Minneapolis by a woman who told me how making a weekly connection with her little girl had made a profound impact on her newly retired father. Six months into his retirement, the family began having concerns and encouraged him to get checked out at the clinic. The diagnosis revealed the initial signs of cognitive impairment, indicating the development of dementia. Everyone in the family had noted the aimlessness that had marked his days since retirement. His daughter, sensing his need for purposeful engagement, asked him if he would be willing to watch her daughter one day a week (the signs weren't significant yet to warrant fear); he enthusiastically agreed. At the time of my talk, this arrangement had been going on for over a year. With misty eyes, his daughter told me that he had recently been to the doctors and all signs of the developing dementia had disappeared. Sometimes an ongoing connection can be a life saver.

Renew

The quest for renewal takes on many unique and individualized forms for every person. For some, it is attending to a hobby that brings them serenity and fulfillment, such as gardening.

For others, renewal means attending to personal growth in areas where they feel a sense of neglect. These can range from taking self-improvement courses, to obtaining new degrees from a university, to embarking on a spiritual pilgrimage, to creating a radical change in one's pace and focus to "try on" a new way of living.

For some people, a period of renewal simply means not working. For these individuals, being free from vocational obligations, schedules, and commutes is the source of their renewing. After a time of chilling, I've seen many of these temporary retirees gain a sense of clarity, centering on what they want to do next. For some, it is a cause they want to engage in, while for others, it is an almost forgotten goal or pursuit they are ready to dust off and make a run at with their newfound energy.

The retirement era focus on renewal is driven by a need for balance, meaning, and peace of mind that many have found lacking in their vocational pursuits and schedules. Some feel they have lost touch with friends and family, some have forgotten how to play, some feel they have lost touch with balanced living and relaxation, and some are feeling the dearth of time to attend to their own interests and inclinations. A major driver in this period of life is about aging well.

In an article titled "Reinventing Retirement: New Pathways, New Meanings," the authors say that for some, one way to resist aging is to keep working; by doing so, mature workers combat invisibility and stay young by staying active. Others reported defying age through active self-work and disciplining the body through exercise and keeping fit.[1]

A whole generation of retirees is learning to resist aging by keeping active and fit. Go to your local health club or gym and note the average age of the participants. According to Club Industry (http://clubindustry.com/), as of the end of 2012, nearly one-quarter of all gym memberships were held by those over 55.[2] Renewal is an important topic for many new retirees as they are hoping to discover how to stay younger due to an increase in their subjective well-being. They are feeding their human needs, thus causing a spillover effect onto other domains in life. Michael B. Frisch defined the 16 areas of life that we all want to elevate our well-being. They are in the list that follows. How would you rate your current state in regard to these 16 areas?[3]

Health	1	2	3	4	5
Self-esteem	1	2	3	4	5
Goals/values	1	2	3	4	5
Money	1	2	3	4	5
Work	1	2	3	4	5
Play	1	2	3	4	5
Learning	1	2	3	4	5
Creativity	1	2	3	4	5
Helping	1	2	3	4	5
Love	1	2	3	4	5
Friends	1	2	3	4	5
Children	1	2	3	4	5
Relatives	1	2	3	4	5
Home	1	2	3	4	5
Neighbors	1	2	3	4	5
Community	1	2	3	4	5

As I look at this list, it is clear that the majority of these items are pretty important to most human beings. The one element that does not elevate to the level of the others in terms of importance in our modern times might be *neighbors,* as it depends on the type of neighborhood or area you live in. If you are in an area with great swaths of space between you and your neighbors, there is a good chance that being neighborly wasn't a great motivation for moving into the neighborhood. But the rest of the list contains elements that most of us will acknowledge have a bearing to varying degrees on our well-being, underscoring the idea that life, at all times, is a great balancing act.

Your own next 100,000 miles will depend on an analysis of what constitutes balance for you (your retirement personality), an assessment of your current level of balance, and an occasional stop at the "re-tire" shop to see how that balance is holding. This retirement era is not an exit ramp; it is an entrance ramp. There is a long adventurous road ahead of you—make sure you get "re-tired."

Individual Retirement Attitude

I realize that today's retirement is not "the end of the road" but the beginning of a new path with many turns and possible detours. Rather than resigning, I will apply new tread and prepare for the next 100,000 miles of my life with an air of adventure and expectation!

CHAPTER 11

Redefining Rich: Bridging the Gap between Means and Meaning

"To allow me to do what I want to do everyday."
—Warren Buffett on the meaning of money

Harry Houdini, the famous escape artist, issued a challenge everywhere he went. He claimed he could be locked in any jail cell anywhere in the country and be able to free himself in a short time. He never failed in this challenge except for one isolated incident. One day Houdini walked into a jail cell and the door clanged shut behind him. From under his belt Houdini removed a strong but flexible piece of metal. He began to work, but something seemed odd about this particular lock. He worked for 30 minutes with no results. Frustrated, he labored for another hour and a half. By now he was soaked in sweat and exasperated at his inability to pick this lock. Completely drained from the experience, Houdini collapsed in frustration and failure and fell against the door. To his surprise, the door swung open—it had never been locked! The door was locked only in the mind of Houdini.

We would all do well to pause for a moment from our heated labors and lean against the philosophical door that can free us from feelings of futility, frustration, insignificance, and even failure. We lean against this door by asking ourselves what we must do to bring a greater sense of meaning to the means we gather in our working lives. Once that door is opened, everything else, including our material management, can be ordered in such a way as to accelerate and accommodate a more meaningful existence.

In this chapter, my goal is to reframe the conversation around building wealth toward *living rich,* as opposed to simply getting rich. One is a state of contentment and purposeful being, and the other is a discontented chase that never ends; there simply is no exit ramp. A friend of mine who works with ultra-wealthy people in a major metro area conducted a survey that asked, "How much money would you need to have to consider yourself rich?" Those with $25 million said the number was $50 million. Those with $50 million said the number was $100 million. Those with $100 million said the number was $200 million. The first group who would admit that they were already rich were those with $200 million dollars.

In many respects, you could take the preceding illustration and plug in the numbers you want ($250k to $500k to $1,000,000 or $1M to $2M to $3M), and you will get the same existential conclusion: discontentment is hardwired into the culture and attitude of the majority. If you can find contentment wherever you are, you already know that you're "richer" than those who have the means but lack the attitude to enjoy what they have gathered. Our perceptions around what money can and can't do for us have a great bearing here, as does facing the reality that more money can also mean more stress and more responsibility.

A study by the Spectrem Group said wealth meant "greater security." Ranking a distant second place was "more happiness," followed by "more responsibility," and "more fun." Ranking last was "more stress." The results of these perceptions are skewed by both the age and net worth of the respondents. Older respondents were more likely than the younger respondents to say that being rich meant security. The older the investor, the more likely they were to say that wealth brought more responsibility and a more complicated life.[1]

The more money you have, the more likely you are to associate wealth with security and responsibility. Corporate executives are more likely to associate being rich with "more stress." The author of this study concluded: "Americans have a pretty good sense of what wealth can—and more importantly—cannot buy. Yes, it brings a certain form of security and fun; but it also brings more responsibility, stresses, and complications. Wealth doesn't erase life's problems: it just replaces them with more expensive ones."

We live in a world that is obsessed with increasing ROI (return on investment) when we should be more concerned with achieving ROL (return on life). "Return on life" is a phrase I developed to define the ultimate purpose of gathering and investing materially. No one gathers only for the sake of gathering. Even the greedy and acrimonious have an extra-material purpose for gathering, whether it is conceit, power, or extreme insecurity. We'll talk more about the specifics of ROL in the next chapter.

The first question that should be asked and answered in a money management conversation is not "What kind of return are you hoping for?" but rather "What is the money for?" The end objective should inform all decisions that are made around the management of your means. Meaning leads the wagon instead of following it. We don't live purposefully by expending everything we have toward gathering the most money possible, and just hope that something meaningful happens on the way. We live purposefully by *investing on purpose*—deciding up front why we want the money, and deploying those means in a fashion that fuels meaningful pursuits.

Another perspective we hear too little of is that the focus on building wealth is not without consequence. A study by U.S. Trust on Wealth and Worth found that two-thirds of respondents said they didn't take enough time off, half said they didn't have enough time for family, about a third said they were defining their self-worth by their wealth, and a quarter admitted they were mishandling relationships in their pursuit for wealth. Clearly, we need to count the cost of chasing bigger numbers. For some, the bottom line is that they can ill afford the wealth they seek.[2]

> *Money is a terrible master. If it gets over you and you get under it, you become its slave.*
>
> —E. Stanley Jones, theologian

In the course of asking people what gives meaning to their lives, I often hear such answers as happiness, fulfillment, balance, satisfaction, security, significance, and success. When people use these words, are they simply using different terms to talk about the same thing, or do their answers reveal unique elements to a meaningful life? I believe they are unique elements that, once understood for what they are, will add a great degree of clarity to their lives. Success is not the same as significance. People can be enormously successful by world standards and feel that what they do is not significant. Happiness can easily be differentiated from security, and it is possible to have one without the other.

As we look forward to a meaningful transition in our lives, we need to understand how these seven elements together can define a meaningful and contented life. A meaningful life is a life full of meaning. The conversation around money matters should not exclude meaning, but rather meaning should be placed at the very center of the money conversation: *How can I get the most meaning from my means?*

There are many aspects of our lives that give us a sense of fulfillment—family, achievement, exploration, freedom, and altruism are some of the more important ones. For the sake of clarity, I would like to make an attempt at defining these seven meaningful intangibles. Many times, people can have a personal epiphany when they come to understand these goals for what they are and stop looking for them in the wrong places.

The Seven Intangibles

> *"No trumpets sound when the important decisions of our life are made. Destiny is made known silently."*
>
> —Agnes de Mille

Happiness Is Wanting What You Already Have

This is not the Madison Avenue definition of happiness. In fact, this definition is the polar opposite of Madison Avenue's mantra that "happiness is having more than you have now." This old and worn sermon is one we have heard a million times: things won't make us happy. Yet we watch the ads and begin to accept the underlying message that possessions define the person. Shortly after the invention of the coin in ancient times, the Greeks came up with the phrase *Oremata Aner,* which, when translated, is "Money is the man." It didn't take long after the invention of what we call *money* for it to become a metaphor for much more than the ore it was composed from. It soon became the measure of a man's abilities, his value, his skill, and ultimately his worth. Has this changed over the centuries? Hardly.

If anything, the message has only been further imprinted into the soul of mankind, ultimately establishing money as the religion that rules secular existence. We begin to develop a keen sense of peripheral vision regarding our neighbors' homes and the possessions filling those homes. Soon, we too have assumed the definition of happiness that Madison Avenue has designed for us: "The more you have, the happier you'll be. You really won't be happy until you get the things you want." *Oremata Aner* is the mantra of Madison Avenue's efforts.

But the true key to happiness is not in getting those things; it is in changing what you want. If you cannot sense the emotion of contentment with your current circumstances, what makes you think you will feel it with your desired circumstances? Your desired circumstances will only change your view. Once you get there, you will be subjected to a whole new and higher realm of advertising proclaiming that you can have more than this.

How money makes you feel and influences your perspectives in life often depends on how much or little you have. Money offers arrogance to the "haves" and shame and envy to the "have-nots." There is the voice that asks, "What do you suppose he or she is worth?"—as if the answer to that question will make the difference in our assessment of them as a person. Who's better? A good guy who's loaded or a good guy who's scraping by? Isn't being a good guy enough to warrant admiration?

> *"Money won't make you happy, but neither will poverty."*
>
> —Warrren Buffett

These comments are not pious rantings against possessions and a home on the hill. Possessions can be personal rewards for significant labors—and there is certainly nothing wrong with rewarding your efforts. Where many individuals go wrong, however, is in believing that things, once possessed, will make them happy. Ultimately, they will not. In fact, as many of those who possess the things you may think you want will tell you, these things have the potential to make you unhappy because all things of value require responsibility and insecurity. A bigger house means more work, more maintenance, and more things that can go wrong—at a bigger price tag. Part of the price tag of that shiny new car, boat, or other luxury item is insecurity, because now there is worry about damage and risk.

An important resolution to settle is that happiness is a state of mind and not a state of material ownership. If we do not settle this fact, we are destined to a maze of futility at a very high price.

> When I started making really good money, I decided to buy myself a really nice watch, something in the Rolex genre. In the midst of my search, I stopped myself with the thought that I wasn't really being honest with myself as to why I wanted this watch. I came to the conclusion that the motive I was articulating didn't agree with what I was feeling. I said I wanted the watch because "I wanted a nice-looking, dependable timepiece." But what I was feeling inside was that I simply wanted to impress others with my achievements. I asked myself if I really needed to spend $7,000 to tell everyone I had made it. I thought of some of my family back home who wouldn't know a Rolex from a Timex. I came to a compromise. I decided I did indeed want to reward myself with a fine timepiece but that I would not choose a brand that was a blatant advertisement of my achievement. I bought a brand every bit as beautiful and dependable as a Rolex but far less recognizable to the masses. This decision started a very powerful line of reasoning that, so far, has kept me from buying a bigger house and more expensive car than I really need and has helped to keep my materialism in check. It's like the old saying, "We buy things we don't need with money we don't have to impress people we don't like." And I'm trying not to go down that path.
>
> —Doug, insurance executive

Happiness is easy. Don't complicate it. If you want what you have, you are happy.

Fulfillment Is Optimizing the Use of Your Abilities

Fulfillment is easy, too. It is doing the things you love to do. It is expressing your working soul. It is engaging in work that energizes you rather than depletes you. Fulfillment does not necessarily come from success in the career you are in, if that career is not the soul-felt expression of who you are. When you are expressing who you are with your work, you have shaken hands with fulfillment. Once you discover this relationship between who you are and what you do, it is awfully difficult to go back to work that engages the hands but not the heart. Taste this water, and you will no longer be satisfied with simply making a living.

I remember well the lack of fulfillment I felt at one point in my career because I was doing the same routine over and over. I knew I needed an outlet for the creative impulse within me. I wasn't fulfilled until I found ways to express that creativity. I now know that I can never go back to the kind of work that clogs the creative impulse urging me from within. My first criterion today when I am offered work is not how much I'll make but whether it will be a creative challenge. Once you discover the work that fulfills you, it will be hard, if not impossible, to disengage yourself from it.

Balance Is Walking the Tightrope between Too Much and Not Enough

Work, family, and leisure—when we get them in balance, we enjoy life. Feeling as if we're having fun in life is a good indicator that we have achieved some degree of balance. How many people do you know who have worked hard for so long that they no longer know how to relax when they get the opportunity? How many people do you know who are so busy supporting their family that they never see their family? What do they achieve by neglecting the very people that motivate them to earn a good living? People today are aware of these issues and are no longer as willing to put their personal life in a deep freeze for the sake of their company's goals. It is becoming quite frequent in interviews to hear the applicant ask, "Will I have a life?" A growing percentage of employees are willing to trade more income for more time and flexibility, even during tough economic times.

At the other extreme of the life balance pendulum are the individuals who have so much time for leisure that they have lost their sense of purpose and significance, and, consequently, their fun is no longer fun. There is a fine balance to be achieved in attending to the physical, emotional, social, and spiritual sides of our being. There is also a fine balance to be achieved in attending to the working, familial, and frolicking sides of our being.

Satisfaction Is Improving the Quality of Your Efforts and Relationships

Satisfaction is a quality issue. If you are constantly seeking to raise the level of quality in the products and services you are involved with, if you are constantly striving to improve key relationships in your life, and if you are living a thoughtful, self-examined life, you will feel a sense of satisfaction.

When talking to those who feel a sense of dissatisfaction in their life, I see a recurring pattern of lukewarm relationships and lack of conviction about the impact and meaning of their daily work. It is important to look for opportunities to satisfy your need for inner satisfaction at the place you are today before you start believing greener grasses elsewhere will fill that appetite. I recently talked with a woman who told me she needed to get back to helping the homeless so she could feel a greater sense of satisfaction about her life. She felt her life was too self-absorbed. I asked her what she did in her job to help others. She thought about it and said that she gave seminars helping women discover financial independence. After she said that, she suddenly realized she was ignoring a great source of inner satisfaction right under her nose. Satisfaction can often be fulfilled by appreciating the things we do now and by striving to do them better. By raising our eyes to a standard of excellence in our efforts we raise our levels of satisfaction. Satisfaction revolves around the quality of our efforts and our relationships.

Security Is Possessing the Freedom to Pursue Your Goals

Whether our goals are anchored in work, family, leisure, or all of the above, we feel a sense of security only when we know we will have the freedom to continue pursuing those goals. People may feel insecure about their job for fear of getting laid off and not being able to pursue the work goals they desire. Others fear they will not have enough assets to be able to pursue the lifestyle they want in their retirement years. Possessing adequate finances can unquestionably provide a degree of security because it can offer a material guarantee, of sorts, that we will be able to do what we want with our lives. This is the security that modern retirement represents for most people. Life will always present us with opportunities to feel insecure because very little in this world is guaranteed. We may have the money to do what we want, but our health could diminish and rob us of our mobility and activity. We can make all sorts of plans for the future, but we have no guarantee that those plans will pan out.

Security hinges on more than just the health of our assets; it is also affected by the health of our body and close relationships.

As billionaire Warren Buffett put it, "The only two things that can make you truly happy in this world are people that love you and being healthy, and money can't buy you either one of those." We can, however, build on our sense of security by staying close to those who love us, forming good physical habits, and continuing to put away all we can toward our financial emancipation.

Significance Is Making the Best Use of Your Time

Viktor Frankl stated that man's chief motivation was the need for significance. People are motivated by a need to make a difference somehow in others' lives—to feel they are making a contribution that is significant. Many people erroneously believe that a sense of significance will be satisfied by the acquisition of power and control over others. It cannot. This inward sense of significance is satisfied by the best possible use of our most valuable resource: time.

We all have only so many days on this Earth, and those days are fleeting. Look at how quickly the last decade has seemed to pass. Parents get a magnified perspective on the fleeting nature of time as they watch their children sprout and exit, while they feel almost the same as they did 15 years ago. People want to make a difference in other people's lives. People want to make a difference in the work they do. People want to make a difference with the wise distribution of their time, energy, and resources. Money has the power to feed this significance only when it is shared or emancipates us to share our time and skills. Charity and volunteerism can be crucial to a sense of significance in our lives.

A person who works in a job but doesn't see the benefit of that job to the end usually will lack a sense of significance. He will feel that he is wasting his time. A person who is a workaholic and misses all her children's meaningful activities will feel that she is abusing the short time she has. Significance is closely related to how we manage the time we have.

Success Is the Satisfaction of Reaching Your Goals

Success is a sense that relies heavily on moving toward or achieving personal goals. But the term *success* must be broadened beyond the material to have real meaning in life. Truly successful individuals have goals involving who they are (character), what they do (career), and what they possess (material)—and, more than likely, in that order of importance. How successful does an individual who is garnering riches but failing in the personal character department feel? Certainly, one's reputation is worth its weight in gold. Financial success could be defined as having enough to meet your own needs and the needs of those you choose to help. This is a worthy financial goal.

Career success could be defined as having the opportunity to pursue one's career goals. We feel most successful when we are actively pursuing our heartfelt goals. As long as we are actively pursuing personal goals and making progress toward them, our sense of success and confidence will be fed.

A sense of success starts with first having a goal. Many fail the financial success test at this point because they have not clearly defined financial goals. Having enough to retire is not a goal; it is a vague desire, a dream. Wanting to have financial assets of half a million dollars by the time you are 60 is a clearly articulated goal. Now you have a standard against which to measure your success. Having a clearly defined goal to feel successful holds as true in your career and character as in your finances. Studies show that the majority of people do not have clearly defined financial goals, and I would assume this to be true in other areas of life as well. In the financial realm, this problem can be easily remedied by partnering with someone who can first help you articulate those goals and then help you stay the course in achieving those goals.

These seven intangibles cannot be satisfied by a certain amount of material possessions or by a number. Happiness, fulfillment, balance, satisfaction, security, significance, and success should not be the by-products of life; they should be the goals! Having these seven intangibles present in our souls is the very definition of rich living in spite of the amount of our investable assets. When we myopically focus on money instead of meaning in our lives, we deny ourselves the fulfillment that we could garner both from our means and our time. Remember, your life is not about making money—*your money is about making a life.* These seven intangibles cannot be bought, but you can easily sell them out.

The Stewardship of Money

My deepest conviction regarding the topic of important conversations around money is that the conversation is not complete until we examine our relationship to money in the light of stewardship.

A definition of the word *steward* is a person whose responsibility is to take care of something: *farmers pride themselves on being stewards of the countryside.* Stewardship is the transcendent realization that although material wealth is in our care, we are responsible—it is never really "ours." The money is passing through us as if we were conduits.

We don't achieve financial/life success by engaging in a numbers-only money discussion, hoping that it fits our lives. We experience financial/life success by taking a closer look at our lives—what we are experiencing, what we hope to experience—and by designing a financial plan around those life factors. What can you do to make a meaningful and resourceful transition in your life? You can begin this transition by following these three steps:

1. Decide what is *meaningful* in your life.
2. Begin looking at innovative ways to use your resources (money, time, and ability) to purchase the life you want.
3. Partner with those people who can help you articulate and achieve your goals.

Ultimately, living "rich" is about aligning your life and money—by placing meaning at the center of each financial decision. It is what I call *investing on purpose.* Once you adopt this approach, you may find a new sense of wholeness and peace surrounding your financial and investment decisions because you are engaging in *a unifying philosophy of life that defines purpose for your money and, consequently, your life.*

Individual Retirement Attitude

No other human can define "rich" for me. I will manage my resources wisely and with an eye toward extracting the most meaning from the means I possess. My focus will be to achieve ROL, return on life, by living the best life possible with the money I have.

Moving from ROI to ROL (Return on Life)

"Some people know the cost of everything but the value of nothing."
—Oscar Wilde

In writing about the characteristics of healthy personalities, the late Dr. Gordon Allport of Harvard fame, offered these six traits:

1. A positive concept of self.
2. Seeing value in people as human beings.
3. Enjoyment in helping others.
4. A realistic perception of the world.
5. A sense of humor.
6. A unifying philosophy of life that defines purpose for living.

I can't help but wonder when considering these characteristics how much bearing our disposition toward money has on the health of our personalities. For example, do you have a poor self-image because you feel you don't make enough money or manage money well? Have you ever met individuals who, rather than valuing people as humans, view relationships as stepping stones on the path to material achievement? Have you ever wanted to help someone but couldn't afford to? Do you know anyone who is living a champagne lifestyle on a seltzer budget? Has your sense of humor been dampened by financial frustration and strain? And, finally, do you ever feel that your financial situation is keeping you from fulfilling your sense of purpose in life?

Most of us, at one time or another, can probably answer "yes" to one or more of these questions. The quality-of-life issue I'd like to focus on here is the last factor cited by Allport—*a unifying philosophy of life that defines purpose.* In the past decade of observing people's approaches to investing, I have witnessed a great disconnect between their money and their lives. As a result, I sense the need for a unifying dialogue that I define as *Financial Life Planning.*

Financial Life Planning addresses the uniqueness of each of our life issues as they relate to investments and other financial decisions. Too often, we deal with money issues in a quantitative vacuum and leave the life ramifications to chance.

All of our financial or investment decisions should be made based on how it can and will implicate our lives as a whole. On the other side of the financial/life coin, life decisions should not be made without contemplating the impact on our financial situations. There is an umbilical connection between our money and our lives—an inextricable connection where every money decision has the potential to affect the quality of our lives, and every life decision has the potential to impact the quality of our financial situations.

> *"Jesus talked more about money than about heaven. Maybe that's because he understood that money, if not respected for what it is, can turn our lives into a living hell."*
>
> —Mitch Anthony

My first exposure to the need for a unifying discussion around money and life came over 30 years ago as I counseled on a suicide prevention line in Iowa for farmers who had lost their farms. Unlike losing a job, losing the farm amplified the grief because the farmer also lost the legacy of generations that had worked that land.

I talked with many such farmers, and their hurt was real and vivid. They were shocked, embarrassed, pained, and often lost as to their identity. This was happening at a time of historically high interest rates and land values. They had borrowed large sums at rates as high as 20 percent, and those loans had liens against acres assessed at inflated values. When the land values fell (much like the housing crisis that followed), the bubble burst.

Men who had only thought of raising crops were now lifting nooses in their lofts and telling me about it on the phone. Fortunately, we talked scores out of this devastating action, but I was left with an indelible lesson that has underscored my work around money and money issues. The moral of the story for me was that every one of these people was in this existential dilemma for one simple reason—a poorly informed financial decision!

If these individuals had had someone in their lives to counsel their financial choices (other than the people profiting from them), they may well have resisted the urge to overextend themselves, avoiding the devastating circumstances they found themselves in. The first question we need to answer is, "How could this money decision ultimately affect my life, positively or negatively?"

We don't achieve financial/life success by engaging in a numbers-only money discussion, hoping that it fits our lives. We experience financial/life success by taking a closer look at our lives—what we are experiencing, what we hope to experience—and by designing a financial plan around those life factors. In this chapter, we discuss how you can align your life and money. Once you take this step, you may find a new sense of wholeness and peace surrounding your financial and investment decisions *because you are engaging in a unifying philosophy of life that defines purpose for your money and your life.*

A New Measure of Success: ROL

If I were a client and the financial professional I went to visit asked me in the first five minutes about what I had and where it was, I would run for the exit, because it is obvious that that advisor is more interested in my money than in me.

—Roy Diliberto, CFP, selected as one of America's top financial planners by several consumer financial magazines

We, as a culture, are in need of a new standard of success regarding our financial lives. The current standard of return on investment (ROI) is self-limiting and adds pressure to our lives that is counterproductive. What if the markets have a bad year? Should I worry myself sick and loathe my existence? Why do others seem to be getting better returns than I am? Should I beat myself up over it and think I'm unlucky with money?

So much of ROI is out of our control. We can properly diversify. We can be industrious about saving and investing. We can avoid greed and foolish schemes, but we cannot control the behavior of the markets or the world and cultural events that affect the markets any more than we can control the climate patterns around us.

Instead, the standard for financial success should be what I define as *return on life (ROL)*, which is expressed as, *"How well are you doing on living the life you want with the money you have?"* Implied in the ROL approach to life are the following ROL indicators:

- I'm living well within my means.
- I'm saving with discipline.
- I'm managing my risks with prudence.
- I'm investing time, energy, and resources in people and engagements that energize me.
- I'm allowing myself to have experiences and live whenever possible.
- I'm not comparing my progress to others who live with a different set of circumstances.
- I'm living purposefully.
- I'm not allowing my identity to be defined by numbers.

If a picture is worth a thousand words, then a metaphor is worth a thousand pictures. That is true of the preceding metaphor regarding money and life. Have you ever felt like the gerbil on the activity trap with money waving in front of you, telling you to run faster but sensing no real progress?

We all have felt that way at one time or another.

The second illustration is a metaphor representing the ROL view of money. Money is viewed only as a utility to help us navigate where we want to go in life; instead of money controlling us, we control it. We are not slaves to the sail, but we keep our hands on the ropes. Our grip is only as tight as the circumstances required at the time. In seeing the money as a utility, we see what it is not. It is not the shore we travel toward. It is not the sea we travel upon. It is not even the vessel that transports us. It is nothing more than a utility (like the sail) that must be skillfully utilized (in all climates) to keep us moving toward what really matters in our lives.

With ROL, we don't give the best of life or the best parts of ourselves just to get money. The money is there to serve our lives, not vice versa. Millions feel as if life is about little more than "getting ahead." "Getting ahead of what?" is my question. Getting ahead of an artificial definition of success? Getting ahead of your neighbors and coworkers? Getting ahead of where you are now? Getting ahead of someone else's definition of what a successful life ought to be?

There are many in our culture suffering from what I call *half-fluence*—they have some degree of money but not the life they thought would come with it. They missed something along the way, and that something was how to get a greater return on life. The best financial discussion we will ever have with ourselves is to ask, "Who and what really makes me happy in life?" and then arrange our finances to keep those people and experiences front and center in our life.

The Money/Life Puzzle

For more than 10 years I have taught and trained competent and caring financial planners to engage in this life-focused dialogue as a preface to financial planning—and they have profound stories to tell. Many of their clients are experiencing life-changing epiphanies when they engage in dialogues that cut to the core of what money is all about—quality of life and a sense of purpose.

Elizabeth Jetton, CFP, of Atlanta, shares a beautiful metaphor of this unifying philosophy of money and life: "You have a 200-piece jigsaw puzzle scattered on the table in front of you. What is the first and most important piece?" Most people will say the corner piece. Elizabeth answers, "No, it's the picture on the cover of the box. If you don't know what that picture is, you're just moving pieces."

Too often, when it comes to our financial lives, we fail to step back and look at the big picture. Instead, we move pieces around, replacing investments, insurance policies, debts, purchases, and the like, all the while paying too little attention to long-term and holistic perspectives.

The general public has been universally informed that every money issue should and can be solved through a myopic focus on mathematics: "Let's take your age, the amount of money in your portfolio, run some calculations, and presto! Here's the answer for your life." With this approach, if that number is out of your reach, you're all but doomed regardless of your individual goals or circumstances. The financial services industry and its practitioners share some responsibility for this perception (along with the media), as too often they rely exclusively on calculators to solve problems that are better weighed by conscience.

The overweighting on quantitative factors results in a process that is skewed more toward *what we have* instead of *where we are* and *who we are*. How do we begin to balance the books between quantitative and qualitative factors in developing a financial plan? By engaging in Financial Life Planning.

The goal of quantitative inquiry is to establish objectives as expressed in mathematical terms (i.e., amount needed, return expected, time needed, time for accumulation, etc.). Don't get me wrong—these calculations are necessary and good but are not "waterproof." They work only if we have also performed sufficient *qualitative* inquiry into what is going on in our lives and the financial needs arising from that inquiry.

The Core of Financial Planning—Life at the Center

In the traditional financial planning model (Figure 12.1), the primary components include asset management, risk management, debt management, tax planning, estate planning, and income planning. Although each area is meaningful and critical to financial well-being, there is an underlying assumption inherent in the solely quantitative approach used to perform these functions. The tacit and unwitting assumption communicated by many financial professionals in developing a financial plan is that everyone is essentially the same, and the only thing that really needs to change from one person to the next is which numbers get plugged into the formula. Is this an assumption you would want someone to make about you?

As good as your principles and philosophy of money management may be, I am not comfortable with the assumption that my values and principles with money are the same as everyone else's. Neither am I comfortable with the assumption that my history, present circumstances, and future hopes are the same. Yet, by virtue of a process that leans exclusively on mathematical function, these assumptions are made thousands of times a day across the financial planning landscape.

The most important aspect that can come out of the numbers is that they deliver the quality of life that I desire. The numbers do not exist to drive the life but to support it. If we believe this, we

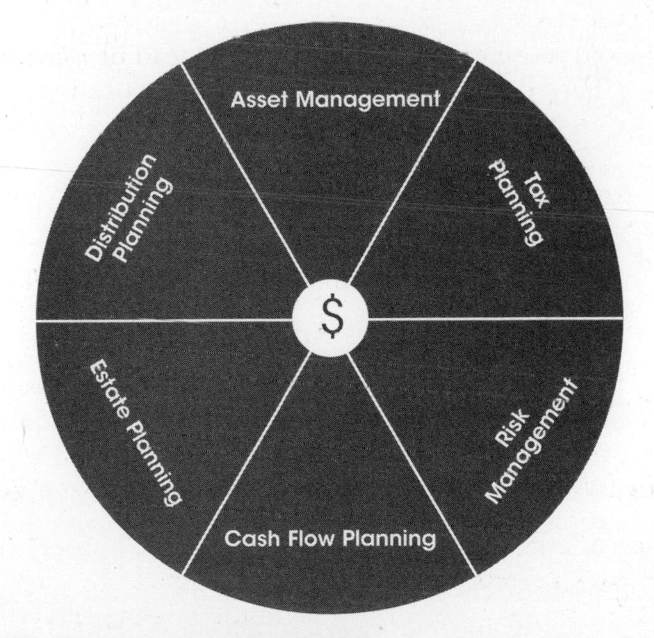

Figure 12.1 Financial Planning Model

must place the primary emphasis on life issues before we address our financial issues. This, in a nutshell, is what Financial Life Planning is all about.

Issues for Our Middle Years and Beyond

Now we come to all the issues that will accompany our progression into our middle and later years. We may never fully retire, but we will, nonetheless, still need to deal with these issues. Because most people have been presented with retirement as only an economic cliff from which they will jump once they're in their 60s, they have only looked at carrying a fiscal parachute. Does this sound like you? In fact, most of us have done only sketchy work on the financial issues and little or no work on all the life issues that will accompany such a transition. The New Retirementality is about your money *and* your life. Life eventually takes us through some very predictable phases. The phases I refer to are borrowed from author Michael Stein: the "go-go" phase, the "slow-go" phase, and the "no-go" phase.

- The "go-go" phase is like the second childhood (one author called it "middlescence"), the time when, if you achieve your financial emancipation, you can do all the things you wanted to do but couldn't because you were too busy working. Stein characterizes this period as "a second childhood without parental supervision, potentially the most wonderful time in a person's life."
- The "slow-go" phase is a more passive phase that is marked by time for more quiet introspection and getting life straight.
- The "no-go" phase is defined by the need for medical and possibly nursing care.

There is no guarantee that we will spend any certain amount of time in these particular phases, but chances are we will end up with experience in all of them. My personal fantasy is that I will live the rest of my life somewhere between the slow-go and the go-go and die in my sleep at 99 (or die of a heart attack at that age from the excitement of a hole-in-one).

I would prefer to live out my emancipated years at a pace that is both challenging and enjoyable, somewhere between go-go and slow-go. If the slow-go years were marked by introspection and increased spirituality, I would prefer to experience them in my current phase of life. It would seem to be a critical step to slow one's pace to a degree if there is a desire for balanced living. From my conversations with those closer to the last phase, it has become apparent to me that I must ponder the possibility of spending both some time and money in the last phase (no-go). At some point, we'll have to make contingency plans. These contingencies include long-term-care insurance, in-home care, and the like.

When we achieve emancipation, we will live most of that emancipated life somewhere in the slow-go to go-go range, but we will still be confronted with issues that come with retirement. These issues are manifold and include the following:

- How we best spend our time and energies.
- How we address our personal health and well-being.
- How we continue to challenge ourselves.
- The role we play in our parents' and/or children's future.
- The kind of legacy we want to leave.
- Our definition of success.

Individual Retirement Attitude

I will seek to understand the impact of money on every area of my life by engaging in a Financial Life Planning process that focuses on what's happening in my life, adjusted financially to facilitate those happenings.
I will seek to use my money to create a better life.

The Waiting Game: Navigating Social (In)Security

"Life was always a matter of waiting for the right moment to act."
—Paulo Coelho

I haven't met many people in my career who can carry on an engaging and fascinating discussion on the topic of Social Security, but Christine Fahlund, senior financial planner at T. Rowe Price, is the exception to the rule. She understands and can explain (in an accessible way), the labyrinthine options available and the nuances of election at various ages—no small undertaking given the length and confounding content of the Social Security manual.

At T. Rowe Price, Christine and her team designed an approach to help people realize a period in life that they can one day look back on as—to use Christine's description—your "vibrant 60s" and maybe even 70s. Her message is simple: if you want to have more money to spend and more security later, you need to play the Social Security "delay game" as much as you can. T. Rowe Price believes that the most important step you can take regarding Social Security election and timing is to educate yourself so you understand both the short- and long-term consequences of your election date decision. Patience and the willingness to wait is the greatest virtue you can bring to this process.

In the chart shown in Figure 13.1, also designed at T. Rowe Price by Christine and her team, you can see the variety of scenarios available to a couple at various ages and various levels of contributions to their 401(k) plans. The chart assumes $500,000 in combined retirement savings accounts at age 62 and an initial

PRACTICE RETIREMENT®: Balancing Time and Money

Preretirees assumed to be a couple contributing to their 401(k) plans, both age 62 with identical current salaries and work history.
Combined salary if no contributions at 62: $100,000 (i.e., $50,000 each); combined retirement savings at 62: $500,000 (5x salary).

MONEY →

TIME ↓

Retirement Age	Initial Withdrawal Percentage from Portfolio	Annual Social Security Benefits if Initiated at Retirement Age	Qualified Retirement Plan Contributions as Percent of Salary (Age 62 to Retirement Age): 0%	5%	15%	25%
			Annual Salary Net of Contributions (Age 62 to Retirement Age)			
			$100,000	$95,000	$85,000	$75,000
			Annual Income Starting at Retirement Age (Income from combined withdrawals and Social Security benefits)			
62	3.7%	$31,464	$49,964	$49,964	$49,964	$49,964
63	3.8%	$33,087	$52,825	$53,023	$53,417	$53,812
64	3.9%	$35,540	$56,584	$56,997	$57,823	$58,649
65	4.0%	$38,194	$60,616	$61,264	$62,560	$63,855
66	4.1%	$40,920	$64,795	$65,698	$67,503	$69,309
67	4.2%	$44,262	$69,669	$70,848	$73,206	$75,563
68	4.3%	$47,717	$74,739	$76,216	$79,170	$82,124
69	4.4%	$51,244	$79,969	$81,767	$85,365	$88,962
70	4.5%	$54,848	$85,366	$87,511	$91,800	$96,090

All figures shown pretax in today's dollars at age 62, assuming a 3% inflation rate. Preretirement asset growth is 7% annually. Social Security benefits are estimated in "inflated (future) dollars" on the Social Security Administration's web site, ssa.gov (using the Quick Calculator, assuming a 0% relative growth factor), then discounted 3% annually.

Figure 13.1 Practice Retirement: Balancing Time and Money

Source: T. Rowe Price Investment Services, Inc. and www.ssa.gov.

withdrawal amount of approximately 4 percent of the portfolio (adjusted if more or less than a 30 year retirement), along with combined Social Security benefits to come up with the income in today's dollars (i.e., lifestyle) you can expect for the rest of your life.

In the highlighted boxes in Figure 13.1 you can see that if a couple living on a combined salary net of contributions of $85,000 a year elected to take their benefits at age 62 (top highlighted box), their combined Social Security benefit would be $31,464, and their total income would be $$49,964. Were this same couple to decide to continue working, delay distributions and continue contributions until age 70, their income in retirement rises to $91,800 because of the increase in the Social Security benefit (from $31,464 to $54,848) and the compounding of their retirement savings accounts in that eight-year period.

Your income in today's dollars would rise from $50,000 to $92,000, an increase of $42,000. To get an additional $42,000 in income at approximately a 4 percent initial withdrawal amount would normally require adding over a million dollars to your savings! But in this scenario, this couple achieves the additional income by delaying Social Security for eight years. An increase of $42,000 in income is tantamount to giving yourself a raise of 84 percent in eight years. Almost doubling your income from $50,000 to $92,000 a year has great ramifications for one's lifestyle over a 20- to 30-year retirement.

You may be thinking, "I don't want to wait until I'm 70 to get this income." It's a fair enough statement. Then consider the question, "How big a raise would I like, and how long am I willing to delay?" If you follow the column down from the $85,000 net income a year figure, you can see that waiting until age 65 gives you a raise of more than $12,500 (a 25 percent increase), while waiting until age 67 gives you a raise of greater than $23,000 (a 47 percent increase)—these boosts are not easy to dismiss when you consider what you can do with $1,000 or $2,000 more each month. By waiting until 65 you're effectively giving yourself an additional, $1,042 a month ($12,500 divided by 12); by waiting until age 67 it's an additional $1,917 a month ($25,000 divided by 12). The bottom line is that *the waiting game pays.*

Try out the various scenarios available to you by using your own income level and ages at which you would like to take Social Security benefits, and devise a plan that works for you or you and/or your partner's situation.

When Christine gives talks for T. Rowe Price, she describes three different lifestyles for preretirees in their 60s, and she encourages investors to focus on the third of those—which combines working and retiring at the same time.

1. Traditional retirees who want out at 62 and don't care how much less money that exit means. Traditional retirees will have no further contribution and no further earnings.
2. Worker bees who enjoy working so much that they forget about also having fun during those years of their vibrant 60s. Worker bees will have further contributions and further earnings to look forward to—but what about their health?
3. "Practice retirees" who attempt to get the best of both worlds by continuing full- or part-time work and spending money well in their 60s. Instead of working and saving, these practice retirees are simultaneously enjoying their additional years of salary while improving their prospects for the future.

T. Rowe Price shares some additional advice to help regarding retirement income:

- If you have an employer who matches contributions to your 401(k) plan (or other retirement program), never discontinue making contributions—you're throwing away free money.
- People say "no" to the delay game because they have been led to believe—by corporate culture and others—that they are leaving money on the table if they don't start collecting Social Security as soon as they hit 62.
- People choose the early election because they're afraid Social Security won't be there in the future—they want to get what they can while they can. These motivations end up costing many people a good deal of future income since it is unlikely Social Security is going away anytime in the foreseeable future.
- People don't consider the fact that most couples are not the same age—if you are four years apart, the difference should influence your decision on when to start taking withdrawals from your portfolio and receiving Social Security payments. For example, if a spouse is 66 and the other spouse is 62, if they both retire at first spouse's age 66 and start taking

withdrawals and Social Security immediately, in Figure 13.1 the starting annual income for the older spouse would be approximately $34,000 (increased annually for inflation), but the income amount for the younger spouse would only be approximately $25,000, or $9,000 per year less. Given the fact that the retirement time horizon for the younger spouse to reach age 95 would be 33 years instead of 29 years (i.e., 66 to 95), maximizing the couple's income from Social Security while both are alive could be especially important.

- If possible, the higher wage earner in your relationship should wait until age70 to collect because whichever spouse survives will continue getting the bigger of the two Social Security benefits but not both.
- Be sure to start collecting your Social Security when you reach age 70! Christine has met people during her presentations who were over the age of 70, suddenly realizing they hadn't collected Social Security, even though they were entitled.

Risky Business

I was getting my hair cut when I couldn't help but overhear an unusual conversation in the chair next to me. The hairstylist, who appeared to be in her late 20s, was telling her client (who appeared to be around the same age), "Well, I finally moved out of my parents' house and got my own place. It feels pretty good."

"That's ironic," her client replied. "My wife's parents are just getting ready to move in with us. They've fallen on some hard times."

In this ironic twist, we see that not planning ahead carries a great deal of risk. But even if an individual were to plan ahead, he could encounter some unforeseen event with dire fiscal consequences and find himself in just such an unenviable position. This conversation reminded me of another insight Christine Fahlund shared with me: "There are two promises you make to your children, one spoken and the other unspoken:

1. Spoken: "I'll help pay for your college."
2. Unspoken: "I'll never move in with you or ask you for money."

A monetary discussion around retirement is not complete without a discussion of the inherent risks to your fiscal well-being in this stage of life. Yes, it's important to save and to delay distributions as long as you can, but it is also important to keep an eye on the radar of life and be vigilant regarding the obstacles that stand in your way.

Learn to LIVE in Retirement

The four major areas of risk one must navigate during the retirement stage of life are (1) longevity, (2) inflation, (3) volatility (in the markets), and (4) events that threaten one's financial security. These four risks form the acronym LIVE—to live well in retirement, one must navigate each aspect and have a plan for surviving and thriving in spite of the risks posed in each arena.

Longevity

Retirement consultant Dave Zander shared this anecdote with me: "In 1985, Joe retired early at the age of 55 so that he could go fishing. He started receiving a pension check for $652.75 per month. Seven years later he started receiving Social Security. Today, at the age of 85, Joe, who is in relatively good health, is still receiving his pension check of $652.75 each month and continues to go fishing almost every day. What I want to know is this: is Joe going fishing these days because he wants to or because he has to?" The concept of money losing value over time (depreciation due to inflation) is hard for some of us to imagine, but the value of your money over time is directly tied to your personal prospects for longevity. As the following illustration shows, at 3 percent inflation, a dollar is worth about 73 cents in 10 years, 54 cents in 20 years, and 40 cents in 30 years.

At 3 Percent Inflation, $1 Million in Today's Dollars Is Worth:

- 10 years from now: $737,424
- 20 years from now: $543,795
- 30 years from now: $401,007

Inflation

Once people stop earning a paycheck, they begin to pay more attention to inflation and spending power. Issues that seemed less relevant before suddenly take on more meaning: cash flow, rising taxes, inflation, insurance, and more. Many people often aren't mentally prepared for what can be a radical change in their spending habits. When people are not financially or emotionally prepared for a new truth: *the day you stop taking a paycheck, the price of everything matters.*

I was visiting my father in Las Vegas, and we were hanging out in a sports bar. He asked if I wanted to go to a movie we had been talking about. I agreed, and he said, "Let's go to the early afternoon matinee." I thought to myself, "This theater is going to be empty on a Tuesday afternoon at 1 P.M." We walked into the theater, and I was stunned to see almost every seat taken. I turned to my dad with a "what in the world?" look on my face as I viewed a decidedly retired populace awaiting the feature, and he said, "You get $1 off on the Tuesday matinee."

I believe it was William Feather who said the reward of energy, enterprise, and thrift is taxes. The reality people encounter soon enough when they stop cashing a paycheck is that taxes and gas prices continue to rise, while their income may not. At this point the thrift impulse goes into higher gear and can start segueing toward fear or parsimony. We have all witnessed the progression in someone we know.

A practical issue the starry-eyed candidate for retirement often overlooks is the impact of inflation over time. If a 65-year-old has a $2 million nest egg growing annually at 5 percent, she can expect a cash flow of $100,000 per year. Even with this amount of money, when adjusted for 3 percent inflation, its spending power is greatly diluted over time. This is a realistic projection for individuals entering the final quarter or third of their life, especially if they expect their discretionary spending to increase in retirement.

I can remember a picture of Jack Nicklaus on the cover of a sports magazine from about 30 years ago with a headline about his winning $100,000 in a year. Players today win 10 times that in one tournament. What will that $100,000 represent in another 25 years? The poverty line? Who knows?

Volatility

I created an interactive illustration called *Retirement Roulette* that features stock market returns for the past 38 years in the 38 slots that make up a typical roulette wheel. Candidates broaching retirement can enter the amount of their savings and the distribution amount they want to receive each year, and then see their balance at the end of a 10-, 20-, or 30-year period—factoring in market returns along with their withdrawals. The results are totally random. For example, you can start with $1 million, and take out distributions of $30,000 a year, and—at the end of 20 years, you could have $2 million left or be broke by the eighth year, depending on the vicissitudes of the stock market. The exercise illustrates the twists, turns, and inconstancies of the market, and how they result in a wild ride that is not always easily stomached by retirees (or anyone else, for that matter).

The point of the exercise was to squeeze a 20- to 30-year investment journey into a five-minute microcosm of emotion. The experience forces people to rationally consider exactly how much risk they can tolerate without sabotaging their quality of life. For many, the insecurity starts as soon as they submit their resignation from work. They begin obsessing over financial details and investment returns—driving their family and their financial advisor crazy. These retirees now have the time and opportunity to delve into minutiae and become addicted to it. The sudden reliance on investment income as opposed to earned income can quickly trigger such an obsession. Now the dream life of sitting on the beach and drinking mai tais has turned into obsessing over *Investor's Business Daily* and drinking Pepto-Bismol.

Events

Unexpected events or being unprepared for alterations in life tend to get the short shrift in the conversation around risks that are inherent in retirement. Events that are catastrophic, disabling, unplanned for, or merely distracting upset many a retirement mirage. A spouse's illness, a sizable investment loss, financial support for a child or parent, and a divorce or remarriage are all examples of events to be considered in the retirement risks conversation. Many of the "what-if's" can be addressed in the context of insurance coverage and/or estate planning, but far too many people procrastinate or simply ignore the issues until the event is upon them—potentially sabotaging their financial stability. I encourage any person or couple approaching the stage of cessation of paychecks to consider all the possibilities of life and to take a proactive approach. Sit down with a competent and caring financial planner if you're not sure where to start.

Individual Retirement Attitude

It has been said that those who master patience master everything else. I will do my best to continue to receive paychecks for as long as possible and give myself a raise for my future. I will be proactive and creative while I continue working, making sure not to miss out on the fun in my 60s and 70s. In fact, I'll use some of my additional years of income to pay for that fun. I'll do it *my* way.

CHAPTER 14

Maslow Meets Retirement

"Self-actualization is the desire to become more and more what one is, to become everything that one is capable of becoming."

—Abraham Maslow

At the age of 52, Briggs Matsko was about to retire from his financial planning business. A friend heard about Briggs's plans and sent him a copy of this book. Briggs said that reading *The New Retirementality* not only changed his life but also gave him a new passion and mission for the work he thought he was going to leave.

I had the pleasure of meeting Briggs over breakfast while in California on a speaking engagement. He shared this story with me:

> I had a real epiphany when I read your book and realized that the most foolish thing I could do is retire early and go into a life of wondering how to make a difference. The opportunity for making a difference was right there in front of me in every client conversation. I just needed to change the conversation from being a numbers conversation to being a life conversation.

Briggs began by telling clients about his awakening and then giving them a copy of the book to read before they came in for their appointment. He told them to come prepared to discuss the sort of life they were desirous of living before they entered a conversation on what to do with their money. When they came for their appointments, they already were primed to talk about the life they wanted to live.

Briggs has been quite generous in sharing with me some of the testimonials that his clients shared with him as a result of reading the book and engaging in a conversation with him. One client comment to Briggs stands out to me: "I need your help to start living the life I want to live and not wait any longer." This woman realized that she needed a relationship with a financial planner who would invest in her life and help her arrange her finances in a way that would lead to true self-actualization.

The New Retirementality conversation has transformed not only Briggs's life but the lives of many of his clients as well. Briggs quickly realized how hungry people are to enter a dialogue about how to bring their life into balance and stop delaying their dreams. Once this dialogue regarding lifestyle takes place, we are ready to move to the conversation of *how to pay for the lifestyle we desire.* But we are not really ready for the money conversation until we have experienced the dialogue about what we really want from our life. Money can either serve or impede a life worth living.

We first need to figure out what we desire out of life and then how we are going to pay for it—find it first, and then fund it. The idea is not to arrange our finances first and then see if we can find a life within that framework. In fact, it is the opposite—figure out the life you want and organize your financial situation to serve that purpose.

With a desire to facilitate a money dialogue that revolves around what people desire out of life, I created a financial conversation called "Income for Life," where I overlaid Abraham Maslow's Hierarchy of Needs with a financial inquiry. I mentioned this idea to Briggs at our breakfast that morning, and I thought he was going to jump out of his chair. His eyes got as big as the over-easy eggs on his plate, and it was obvious that he just had to tell me something.

"What is it, Briggs?" I asked. "Are you familiar with Maslow's model?"

"One of the first things I did when coming back to work with my new vision," Briggs spilled out, "was to create an income dialogue with clients that I called 'Matsko's Hierarchy of Needs,' where we look at a client's emotional needs before making financial decisions.

I just couldn't resist," Briggs confessed regarding the play on Maslow's name with his own, "with our names being so similar and all."

Briggs had intuitively settled on the same solution as I did after adopting The New Retirementality—an income plan designed to simultaneously settle both emotional and financial ledgers.

Briggs and I had both independently observed that, too often, financial advice and financial planning are based on numbers and strategies outside of the very context they are intended to address: quality of life and a sense of emotional well-being. People cannot simply numbers-crunch their way to emotional well-being and quality of life, but neither can they achieve these ends without crunching the numbers and making the necessary adjustments. There is a need for a Financial Life Planning approach that amalgamates both realms into one conversation.

According to studies by Cerulli and Associates, the greatest fear of Americans isn't dying—it's *living*. People are mortally afraid of living to be 100 and being poor. This socioeconomic anxiety, "bag-lady/poor-old-man syndrome" is deeply rooted in the fear of outliving our money. With the confluence of an aging revolution, rising health care costs, and the erosive power of inflation on our money, it is easy to see how people may not be optimistic about their later years.

As a young man in Iowa, I worked with a social worker named Jeannie to create a charity for widows in our town who were living on minimal food and heat in the winter months. Jeannie discovered the problem by talking to grocery store clerks who said little old ladies were buying dog food, when it was known they did not even own a pet. Jeannie walked the streets, and when she found an older house in somewhat disheveled condition, she would knock on the door and ask to visit. What she found was appalling.

Little old ladies would answer the door in winter months in full winter gear because they had to turn their heat down to 55 degrees or risk having it turned off by the power company for nonpayment. Those who chose to heat neglected to eat, or they ate dog food, as Jeannie stealthily discovered by checking their cupboards. These women were too indoctrinated in Depression-era self-sufficiency to ask for assistance, and so we had to find creative ways to help them (e.g., anonymously paying their heating bills). This experience has stayed with me 30+ years in a visceral way—I don't want to be old and poor. None of us does.

Our Hierarchy of Financial Needs

We will all eventually need to engage in a conversation about developing an income stream that lasts as long as we do, outpacing the inflation that threatens to "rot" our nest egg slowly but surely. To accomplish this task let's begin looking at Maslow's Hierarchy of Needs (with money in mind) and walk through the process of designing an income for life. I have developed a slightly altered financial rendition of Maslow's Hierarchy of Needs for this purpose (see Figure 14.1).

Maslow taught that human beings are motivated by unmet needs, and that lower needs must be satisfied before the higher needs can be addressed. We must meet people's most basic needs (like physical survival) before they will be able to address other needs (like love or actualization). Rather than study rats (like Skinner) or the mentally ill and neurotic (like Freud), Maslow developed his theory by studying people such as Albert Einstein, Eleanor Roosevelt, and Frederick

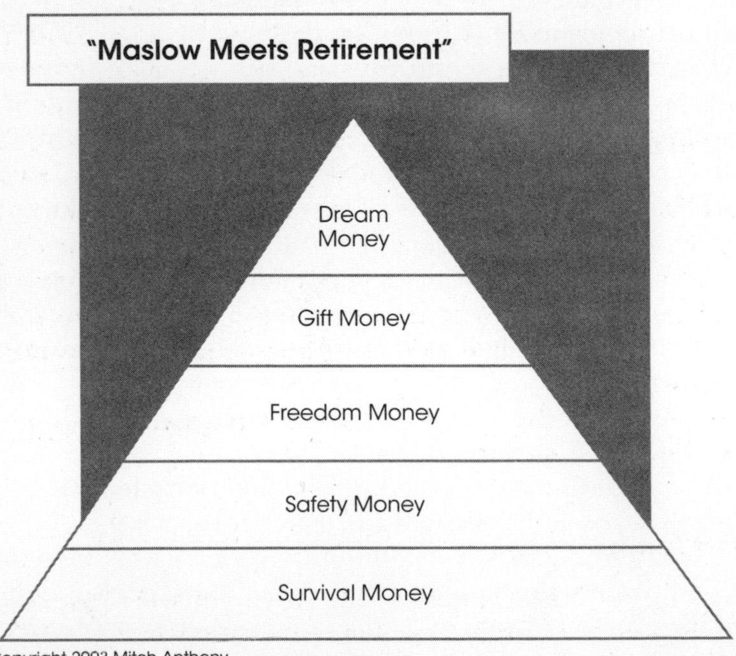

Figure 14.1 Maslow Meets Retirement

Douglas. The hierarchy Maslow offered was physical survival, safety, love, esteem, and self-actualization.

For the purposes of a financial/life discussion, I have taken the liberty of renaming and juxtaposing two categories: love and esteem. Love, in Maslow's definition, had to do with belonging—to a spouse, to a family, to a community, or to a group. For a financial discussion, I have titled this area "gifting," as this is most often the material expression of love.

What Maslow called *esteem*, I have called *freedom* in the financial/life hierarchy. Maslow was referring to the self-esteem that results from doing things well and being recognized for the doing. In the Income for Life model, this is categorized under "freedom money" because unless people have the freedom to do what they want with their occupational lives, they will be missing the esteem and satisfaction that come from doing what they are best at. How many people do you know who long to apply themselves occupationally to something they are naturally good at?

There is also an aspect of financial freedom that allows us to address not just esteem but enjoyment as well. Hobbies and trips and exploration cost money, and if we don't prepare an income stream to address these costs, we may not realize those experiences.

I have placed freedom below gifting on the hierarchy because, from a financial point of view, it is quite unlikely that we will give money away to others *before* we are free to pursue a fulfilling life ourselves. However, there are exceptions to this rule, such as the case of parents who slave at jobs they hate in order to pay for a college education for their children. I happen to believe, however, that it is far healthier—from both emotional and financial perspectives—for people to secure their own freedom to pursue the lives they want. The kids can help with their college expenses by working and saving also.

Following are the phases of financial preparation we need for Income for Life planning.

Survival Income

Survival income is money that we have to have to make ends meet. How much do you need simply to survive each month? $3,000? $7,000? If you stripped away the frills and thrills and just paid the bills of survival, what would it cost? The majority of people have never taken the time to answer this most basic financial question: what is the cost of survival? The money needed to pay for your basic necessities is your survival income.

Safety Income

Safety income is money we must have to meet life's unexpected turns. What if everything doesn't work out as you hoped and imagined it would? In life, the one thing we can predict with great assurance is that things will rarely go exactly as planned. It has been said that "life is what happens while we are making plans." We are surrounded by risks—physical, familial, financial, circumstantial, and relational. Financial risks exist in every category of our lives. Look at the financial risk associated with a divorce—a path that hastens financial ruin, guarantees your assets will be cut in half, and diminishes your saving capacity.

Look at the risk of being disabled for a prolonged period of time. Forty-eight percent of mortgage foreclosures are due to the disability of the chief breadwinner, versus only 3 percent due to the death of the breadwinner. A person who is 35 years old has six times the odds that they will be disabled than the odds that they will die before age 65.[1]

A leading risk in the minds of those individuals approaching retirement is the risk of outliving their money. Other top-of-mind risks are health (and paying for health care), investment risk, loss of income, and financial needs within the family. As much as is possible, we want to protect ourselves against catastrophes to our bodies, our money, and our material things. In many cases, as with our material possessions, this can be accomplished with insurance. It would behoove us all to get an objective opinion on the level of insurance we are carrying toward death, disability, and catastrophe. One incident can wipe out a lifetime of earning. The money needed to guard against these risks is your safety income.

Freedom Income

Freedom income is money to do all of the things that bring enjoyment and fulfillment to life. What is the exact cost of the activities and indulgences that bring pleasure and relaxation into your life? Some people engage in low-cost relaxation activities (like walking), and others engage in high-priced activities (like walking after a golf ball at a private club). Travel, adventure, and personal growth/education are also some of the considerations to include when calculating the amount needed to fund your freedom.

Gift Income

Gift income is money for the people and causes that we care deeply about. As we move up Maslow's pyramid—securing our survival, safety, and freedom—our money can be utilized in the higher calling of bringing blessing to those people and causes we care deeply about. If you are a part of what has been characterized as "the sandwich generation," you are experiencing financial concerns on both ends of the generational spectrum. Many of us would love to do something for our parents *and* our children. Many of us also have aspirations to support causes and charities that connect with our heart and purpose. The money needed to pay for these gifts and benevolent annuities is your gifting income.

Dream Income

Dream income is money for the things we've always dreamed of being, doing, and having. Some would call it their "bucket list" money, borrowing from the movie of the same title starring Jack Nicholson. What do you want to be? What do you want to do? What do you want to have? These are all part of the financial conversation necessary for paying the bills of self-actualization. For some people, only a career change will bring them to this place. For others, it may require part-time involvement in activities more closely aligned with their sense of passion and purpose.

The cost of self-actualization is the time it takes to do the things that bring meaning into our lives. If we do not own enough of our own time to engage in these activities, then we must negotiate with our work schedule and personal finances to make the time available. There is often a cost associated with being what we want to be.

There are also costs associated with doing what we want to do and having what we want to have. Some of us dream of owning a sailboat and spending a year sailing from port to port. Others dream of owning a recreational vehicle and seeing America. Whatever dreams and adventures have surfaced in your own musings on self-actualization, there will be bills to pay in the process. The money needed to pay these bills is your dream income.

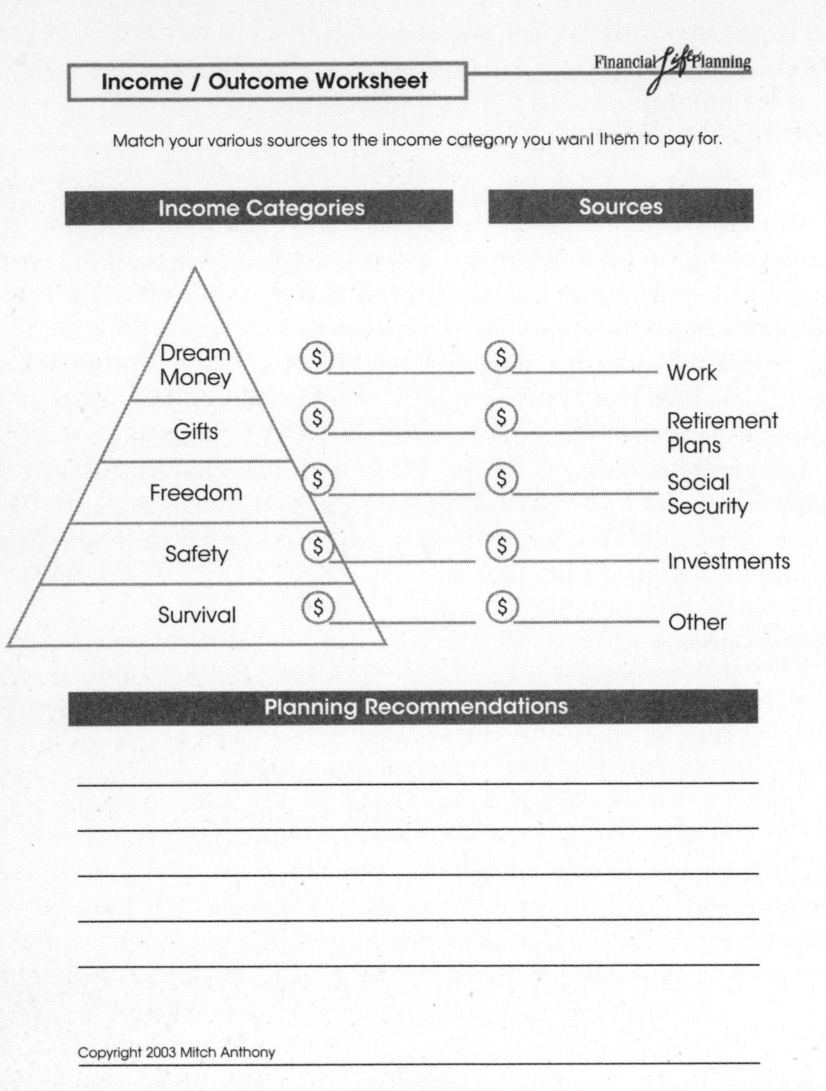

Figure 14.2 Income/Outcome Worksheet

In the next chapter I will introduce you to worksheets you can use to calculate the income needed to live the life you desire. To complete this process (after sorting out all your income needs), you will need to examine your income sources to see how much you can address on Maslow's Hierarchy of Needs and determine the preparations and self-negotiation necessary to cover every level. Potential income sources include income from work, retirement funds, income-earning investments, Social Security, rentals, and/or other sources of income.

Paying the Bills

The final phase of the Income for Life discussion is to match your income sources against your income needs—which sources will pay for which needs (see Figure 14.2). If it's a case of having only enough to pay for survival and safety at this point, then you will at least have the comfort of knowing those two critical bases are covered.

You will also have a clear picture of how much you will need to meet your other needs. You can then set goals around saving and budgeting to expedite achieving the income necessary for funding these important needs of freedom, gifts, and actualization. As one financial planner stated: "If your outgo exceeds your income, you may need to downsize to realize your upside." In other words, if your income isn't enough to meet your needs, you may have to negotiate with your needs.

By working through the exercises in the next chapter, you can bring both clarity and hope into your financial life. Get a handle on what you need and what you have. This exercise produces clarity. Get a handle on what you need to do to get what you want, and how long it will take to get there. This exercise also brings hope. Begin to view your income not as just a way to pay the bills but as a means to funding a life—the life *you* want.

Individual Retirement Attitude

- Develop an income plan that addresses both emotional and financial needs.
- Understand the relationship between being well invested and well-being.
- Order your finances to meet life needs: survival, safety, freedom, love, and self-actualization.

CHAPTER 15

Calculating Income for Life

"There is in the act of preparing the moment we start caring."
—Winston Churchill

We have come to the place where money meets life and heart, where we organize our financial expenses and income sources and attempt to bring them into alignment with the hierarchy of needs we discussed in Chapter 14. By going through this brief financial planning exercise, we can synchronously settle the emotional and financial ledgers.

In this chapter, I have provided simple worksheets for organizing your finances in a way that puts first things first, clarifies what you can and can't pay for at this time, and offers peace of mind for the needs you can meet.

Many people have told me of going through life with a haunting, eerie feeling about their financial lives. They are afraid of those aching questions that never quite make it to the surface of a conversation: Am I walking a financial tightrope with my debt and spending? If my income took a hit, would my lifestyle fall like a house of cards? Is it okay to spend some money to have fun once in a while? Am I really living within my means? Am I going to be financially stressed and miserable in my later years?

Like a lost hiker in the mountains who discovers a global positioning instrument, just discovering where you are brings a degree of comfort—especially compared to the grinding fear in your belly that you are miles from safety. The exercises in this chapter will act like a financial global positioning instrument. You will gain clarity on where you stand with regard to funding your personal survival, safety, freedom, loved ones, and self-actualization. No more wandering and wondering.

Even if this exercise reveals that you still have a ways to go, there is newfound hope in finding clear direction to your destination. It helps you locate yourself.

Paying for Survival

How much money do you need each month to survive? Many of us have a general idea of how much it takes each month to make ends meet; however, making ends meet can include many items outside the purview of survival, such as dining out, club memberships, extra vehicles, and expensive toys.

I was surprised to discover, while conducting Income for Life dialogues, that the majority of people (over 80 percent) had never bothered to calculate their "survival" expenses. Top financial planners across the country have affirmed that because of disorganization, lack of initiative, or just plain denial, most people wouldn't think of calculating survival costs unless they were suddenly put in a position where survival was an issue (e.g., loss of a job with no good prospects on the horizon).

Some people act like they aren't sure they would want to know. Like someone with a nagging pain resisting a doctor's appointment, it may just be too depressing to find out. But after calculating survival costs, most people feel illuminated and relieved knowing the minimum amount it will take them to get by. Those who calculate and do not like where they are begin to see the relationship between their chosen survival lifestyle and the stress they are experiencing in their lives. Many of these people become more resolute to take steps to bring peace of mind to their financial lives.

The Good Old Days

Getting by isn't cheap these days. Of course, it all depends on where and how you live. We all remember the days where we got by on next to nothing. The funny thing is, when I converse with people about those days, many say that, although they had less, they felt more content. Even though many were "just surviving" at some point in their life, they felt they had enough.

I called my oldest son when he was at college to see what his survival budget was. He was 21 years old at the time and living in a beautiful cabin on a lake in the boundary waters, a scene many middle-aged men dream of and will pay dearly for in their retirement years. My son informed me that it took a total of $450 a month to maintain this lifestyle (and it wasn't as long ago as you might think). I asked for the details of his monthly survival ledger. They were:

- Rent: $250
- Groceries: $40 (Yes, you read that right—that is *per month.* "How can that be?" I asked. He informed me, "I buy potatoes, onions, flour, and staples, and catch and hunt the rest. We make up big pots of deer stew and we ice-fish with a sense of purpose.")
- Gas: $50
- Utilities: $50
- Bait, beer, and babes (his description): $60

Oh, for the ingenuity, resourcefulness, and contentment of youth. I remember stringing together such an existence myself—surviving off tips from waiting tables over lunch. It was refreshing for me to hear his budget. It highlighted how our modern definition of survival is inflated with luxury. We could get by with much less if we really had to, and even with a breakeven survival cost many thousands beyond my son's, it brings my soul comfort to know that my family and I could survive with much less and still have one another. We will continue to enjoy the existence we have as long as we can, but there is solace in knowing we could be content in a place where we may never have to go.

Like me at his age, my son dreamed of someday having a new(er) truck, a house to call his own, a spouse, and children after that. Today, he has all that and his survival costs have escalated, as did the need to earn more. Thankfully, he has heeded my many lessons on debt management, living below his means, and paying his bills on time. Hopefully, he will never talk himself or be talked into a survival budget that strips away the joy of living, the joy of working, and the joy of building for the future.

There is comfort to be found in financial clarity. Take time to fill out the Survival Money Worksheet in Figure 15.1.

Financial Life Planning

Survival Money Worksheet

Home / Utilities / Related Needs		
Description	Monthly Need	Yearly Need
Total		

Food / Health / Medical Needs		
Description	Monthly Need	Yearly Need
Total		

Clothing / Personal Care Needs		
Description	Monthly Need	Yearly Need
Total		

Transportation Needs		
Description	Monthly Need	Yearly Need
Total		

Taxes		
Description	Monthly Need	Yearly Need
Total		

Other Needs		
Description	Monthly Need	Yearly Need
Total		

Monthly Survival Total
Survival Money $

Figure 15.1 Survival Money Worksheet

Discover your financial location in monthly and yearly terms. If you are married, discuss your survival situation (if you believe you both can survive the conversation, that is) and talk about how your current survival budget could be adjusted, should you ever face the prospect of having to do so.

Once you have added up your survival expenses, place the total in the total box at the bottom of the worksheet.

Safety Money

Once you ensure that you can meet your survival needs and those of your loved ones, it is time to think about protecting that survival: The instinct for safety organically follows the instinct for survival ("Me build hut, me build fence around hut to keep out thief and tiger.") Inflation is a thief over time. If you are 50 and live to 100 and inflation continues at the same rate it has for the past 50 years, it will have taken 86 percent of your spending power in the next 50 years. As Figure 15.2 illustrates, predators such as disability or long-term care for a loved one—exposures in our risk protection—are waiting to pounce on us at vulnerable moments in life.

- I get paid to give speeches and have been for the past 30 years. What if tomorrow I lost my ability to speak publicly? How would I replace that income for my family? That is a safety issue.
- Fred's mother is showing signs of decline at 80 years of age. Her home and life savings would be consumed if she were placed in an assisted living facility. This is a safety issue for Fred's entire family.
- Bob has longevity in his genes. His father is 92 and going strong. His mother is 90. His grandparents all lived into their late 90s. Bob's finances, invested as they currently are with his current rate of withdrawal, will disappear when he is 83. This is a safety issue for Bob and his wife.
- Jerry has worked hard and saved a lot of money in his professional career. He is two years from eligibility for his pension. His daughter, a recent college graduate, can't find employment and has no health coverage. If a catastrophic illness or accident should happen, Jerry could be wiped out, erasing the 35 most fruitful earning years of his life. This is a safety issue for Jerry and his wife heading into the next phase of their life.

Financial Life Planning

Safety Survey

Scenario		
I Live Past 100	○ Current Concern	○ Future Concern
Serious Family Illness	○ Current Concern	○ Future Concern
Family Needs in Case of Death	○ Current Concern	○ Future Concern
Concern Parents Need Advanced Care	○ Current Concern	○ Future Concern
Child Needs Financial Assistance	○ Current Concern	○ Future Concern
Uninsured Family Member	○ Current Concern	○ Future Concern
Lose Ability to Earn Income	○ Current Concern	○ Future Concern
Lose Job	○ Current Concern	○ Future Concern
Income Reduction	○ Current Concern	○ Future Concern
Major Home Repair	○ Current Concern	○ Future Concern
Need to Replace Vehicle	○ Current Concern	○ Future Concern
Major Vehicle Rapair	○ Current Concern	○ Future Concern
Other	○ Current Concern	○ Future Concern
Other	○ Current Concern	○ Future Concern

Notes: Gather risk protection quotes to calculate your **SAFETY TOTAL** ________________

Monthly Safety Total

Safety Money $

Figure 15.2 Safety Survey

Many of the safety issues can be addressed through insurance products such as long-term care, health insurance, health insurance supplements, disability coverage, life insurance, and homeowner's coverage. Many people also choose to use insured investments that guarantee their principal and a rate of return that outpaces historical inflation rates to address their long-term income needs such as the possibility of living to 100.

Insurance companies are in the business of helping people manage their risks. Exactly how much risk you can tolerate is up to you. Each of us has a distinct and individual tolerance for risk in his or her life. For the sake of awareness, it's important for every one of us to have a conversation about the exposures and vulnerabilities in our life and in the lives of our family members. At the end of that conversation, we can each decide where we desire protection and, ultimately, how much protection we can afford.

Another factor that impacts your need for safety is whether you feel your best earning years are ahead of you or behind you. If you feel they are behind you or you are currently at your peak, safety will assume a more prominent position in your mind.

How Much Risk?

The fact that people continue to build homes on fault lines proves that everyone is unique in his or her response to risk. Some people are comfortable with the risk of living to 100 and trusting that income will be there, and others are not. Some people are comfortable dealing with aging and long-term-care issues when they arise, while others would rather prepare ahead and remove future exposure. As with all risks in life, we must first acknowledge that the risk is there, then decide how to respond to that risk.

A friend of mine who spent 30 years in the insurance industry put it this way: "No one buys insurance wanting to use it. It's a lot like a plunger—nobody ever buys one hoping they get to use it, but should they ever need one and don't have it, they'll find themselves knee deep in it and wishing they had one then." Risk protection is not something we get excited about having, but according to Maslow it is a basic emotional need in our lives. There is some peace of mind in knowing that, if life or Mother Nature brings adversity, we will be safe.

Go through your Safety Survey worksheet in Figure 15.2 and note where your vulnerabilities exist. Are there cracks in your financial foundation? What coverages do you have in your work benefits? You may need to sit down with an insurance provider to calculate long-term-care, disability, or other coverages. Take the time to calculate the monthly cost of building a fence of emotional safety around your survival.

Freedom Money

What are the things you do that make life worth living? What are the activities and places that bring joy to your life? What is the reward you look to after long hours, weeks, and months at your job?

These hobbies, pursuits, and adventures are the engagements that motivate us and energize us to keep our hand to the plow. Without such weekly, monthly, or yearly rewards, life can become drudgery.

A friend told me about a neighbor, a dairy farmer, who at the age of 48 was diagnosed with cancer of the colon. This man had not taken a single day off, including holidays, in 35 years. My friend commented that his neighbor was, as expected, quite miserable, but in all the years he had known him he had always been quite miserable.

How happy could any of us be without taking a cathartic break in more than 10,000 days? The human species was not made this way: "And, on the seventh day, God rested from all his labors."

I know many people in the cattle business, and they tell me that cows don't take days off—and neither can the people who care for them. Some have been fortunate enough to find people who could fill in for short periods, so they could experience the occasional rest and relaxation. What great dividends short periods in diversion of leisure can pay.

My wife, Deb, and I share a similar philosophy in life—work hard and play hard. My wife's play happens to include horses (I play golf and basketball), and so her freedom bill is a lot higher than mine—but it does motivate me to keep working hard! We both work out of our home and try to work efficiently to leave time for play. The opportunity for fun is a constant motivation in our working life. We treasure our leisure pursuits enough that we will pay the price of labor to ensure that the opportunity for fun is always there.

Adding Up the Fun Bill

The important piece is sitting down and doing the math around your "fun" bill. Too many people are in denial regarding their leisure, travel, and entertainment account, and something important is going to suffer as a result. Cash flow analysis, whether it be the itemization and categorization on your credit card or a full-fledged cash flow analysis with a financial planner, is an important reality check. If you can't afford the fun you're having, then finding less expensive options is your only option. If you can afford the fun you're having, then have at it. It's important to cash some life dividend checks along the way.

Our fun bill can run rather high. A friend once warned me to never get a hobby that eats. I didn't understand his point until I married a horse lover. Horses set off a financial domino effect that simply starts with the purchase of the horse: food and board, training, showing, vet bills, farrier bills (new shoes every seven weeks), horse accessories, truck and trailer to pull said horse, and did I mention horse insurance? Can you tell I like to whinny about the horse bills? I often threaten my wife that I am going to start a new national support group called "Equini-non" for men who love women who love horses.

Not that my fun doesn't cost something as well: a golf membership at a good golf club, the early spring golf outing with the boys, and Titleist Pro V1 balls that I have no business buying given their short life expectancy in my golf bag.

Then there is the family trip each year to our favorite retreat in western Michigan. We decided some time ago after watching how fast the kids were growing up that we needed to make a conscious and perpetual effort at creating some magical vacation memories together.

It all adds up, but in our life it adds up to fun—and balance. We have a sense of balance in our personal and family life that keeps us all looking forward and staying out of ruts along the way. It was well worth the exercise for us to sit down and figure out how much these freedoms are costing us and how we will continue to pay for them.

Free to Grow

For some, freedom money is about more than leisure. It is about the freedom to pursue personal growth and expand their capabilities. These pursuits also come with a price tag, whether it is pursuing a degree, taking language lessons, or embarking on a self-improvement course. These freedom initiatives can also bring great joy into our lives as we sense ourselves expanding and growing. The cost of these pursuits needs to be calculated into our freedom income ledger as well. If intellectual growth is a goal but funds are limited, we'll be well served to explore class offerings at public colleges in our area. Tally up your freedom costs on the Freedom Income Worksheet (Figure 15.3), and calculate the monthly income needed in the total box at the bottom.

Money to Give

Once we pass survival, safety, and freedom in our financial hierarchy of needs, we come to the place of giving to others. This is not to say that we can't do any giving along the way while we pay our bills related to survival safety and freedom. Many people form the "charitable habit" and systematically give 10 percent of their income in tithes to their church, 5 percent to charities, or periodically support causes that come around asking for help.

I believe that the *ultimate intention of wealth* is to eventually give back all that was gathered—and to do this in ways that will improve lives and meet real needs in our world. Naked we came, and naked we will leave. I'm reminded of the old joke of the wealthy man who left an equal third of his wealth to his banker, doctor, and lawyer with the agreement that they would place it in his casket before his burial. The banker and doctor grudgingly dropped in their share and watched with horror as the lawyer dropped in a check for his share. He knew the old boy would have no use for it now. And neither will we one day. Take the case of the McDonald's restaurant fortune left by Ray and Joan Kroc. At the end, all those billions of burgers sold ended up being billions of dollars in the hands of the Salvation Army and other charitable organizations, funding their noble efforts at helping the less fortunate. This is a picture of wealth as it should be.

First People First

Because of the expenses of longer life expectancies for our parents and protracted tenures in retirement for us, it is inevitable that the expenses of our predecessors will take precedence over the

Financial Life Planning

Freedom Income Worksheet

Leisure / Hobbies	Monthly Need	Annual Need	Lump Sum
Club Memberships			
Primary Hobby			
Secondary Hobby			
Other			
Total			

Notes: ______________________________

Travel Adventure	Monthly Need	Annual Need	Lump Sum
Second Home			
Vacations			
Family Visits			
Recreational Vehicle			
Other			
Total			

Notes: ______________________________

Personal Growth / Education	Monthly Need	Annual Need	Lump Sum
Education			
Developing New Skill for Income			
Developing New Skill for Pleasure			
Health and Fitness			
Other			
Total			

Notes: ______________________________

Figure 15.3 Freedom Income Worksheet

expenses of our progeny. After all, our children have more earning years ahead of them. You might also consider the example you set for your children by stepping up and helping your parents, if need be. This is an example they may someday need to repeat.

A financial planner from Asia recently told me that when he sits down to talk with clients in their 40s and 50s, one of their first concerns is creating "pocket money" for their parents. This is the first concern because Asians place a premium on experience and age over youth. Our culture worships beauty and youth—albeit ephemeral beauty and ignorant youth. In Korea, the birthdays most worthy of celebration are the 1st and the 70th. Here, we are supposedly over the hill at 60. Whose hill? Does this mean we expect to go into decline after 60? Many people are still ascending at age 80.

If it has been your habit to set aside money for giving to others, you will find the next step useful. The Gifting Income Worksheet (Figure 15.4) takes into consideration parents, children, extended family, and friends and causes near and dear to your heart. Some issues you will need to sort through, prioritize, and calculate around are:

- Subsidizing a parent's survival or freedom costs.
- Contributing toward children's education.
- Contributing toward children's "getting started" costs (i.e., wedding, first home, etc.).
- Creating income streams for your favorite causes.
- Creating a scholarship fund for youth facing hardships and/ or pursuing careers you are familiar with.
- Giving one-time gifts to a project or cause.

Give While You're Living

My friend, Roy Diliberto, CFP, an exceptional financial planner in Philadelphia, loves to tell the story of a woman in her 70s who came to see him with over $2 million and a cost of living that was minimal. Roy asked her if she was charitably inclined. She replied that she was not. Rather than just letting it go, Roy challenged her to take a closer look at her neighborhood and community and look for areas where her gifts might make a difference right away. In their next meeting, she told Roy she had found three causes she wanted to start supporting immediately. She had a new energy and

Financial Life Planning

Gifting Income Worksheet

	Monthly	Annually	One-Time	Amount
Parents				
Income Subsidy	☐	☐	☐	$ ________
Long-Term Care	☐	☐	☐	$ ________
Purchase Their Home	☐	☐	☐	$ ________
Other ________________	☐	☐	☐	$ ________
Children / Grandchildren				
Education	☐	☐	☐	$ ________
Marriage	☐	☐	☐	$ ________
First Home	☐	☐	☐	$ ________
Other ________________	☐	☐	☐	$ ________
Others				
Support for Family Member	☐	☐	☐	$ ________
Support for Close Friend	☐	☐	☐	$ ________
Other ________________	☐	☐	☐	$ ________
Charities / Causes				
Local Causes	☐	☐	☐	$ ________
National Causes	☐	☐	☐	$ ________
Scholarship Fund	☐	☐	☐	$ ________
Create Scholarship Fund	☐	☐	☐	$ ________
Other ________________	☐	☐	☐	$ ________
Other ________________	☐	☐	☐	$ ________

Notes: ____

____

____

____

Monthly Gifting Total
Gifting Money $

Figure 15.4 Gifting Income Worksheet

excitement in her voice as she described the work of the three causes she had located. Now, many years later, Roy reports that all this client can ever talk about are the causes she supports. She has added a few more to the original three, which has added a new layer of meaning to her own existence.

Roy believes that we make a big mistake when we relegate talk of charitable giving to estate-planning conversations. By doing so, the giver misses out on the joy of giving. The New Retirementality take on gifting is *to be giving while you're living.* Be a firsthand, rather than posthumous, witness to your charity.

Tally up the gifts and income streams you'd like to create. How much will it cost each month or each year? Place your gifting total at the bottom of your gifting worksheet. If you find that you really can't afford to provide monetary gifts, there are plenty of other ways to contribute.

Dream Money

The last income category to evaluate is the expenses associated with our dreams, or to borrow from Maslow, the cost of self-actualization. Self-actualization takes a different form for every individual. Here are some of the dreams I've heard from people:

- Starting and running my own business.
- Taking a year to travel the world.
- Working for Habitat for Humanity.
- Writing a book.
- Going back to school to be trained as an artist, teacher, musician, etc.
- Trying different forms of volunteer work.
- Owning a boat and sailing.
- Restoring old cars.
- Woodworking.
- Giving time and talents to a ministry.
- Teaching English to non-native speakers.
- Taking children and grandchildren on a long European vacation.

The list is as endless as the number of people who dream. The worksheet in Figure 15.5 is about being, having, and doing. We dream to *be* someone. It is that wistful seed that lives unsprouted

Financial Life Planning

Dream Worksheet

If I Had the Money...	Cost
Things I've dreamed of owning:	
Places I've dreamed of going:	
Adventures and goals I've dreamed of accomplishing:	

Notes: Research costs associated with your dreams and goals to calculate your **DREAM TOTAL.**

Monthly Dream Total

Dream Money $

Figure 15.5 Dream Worksheet

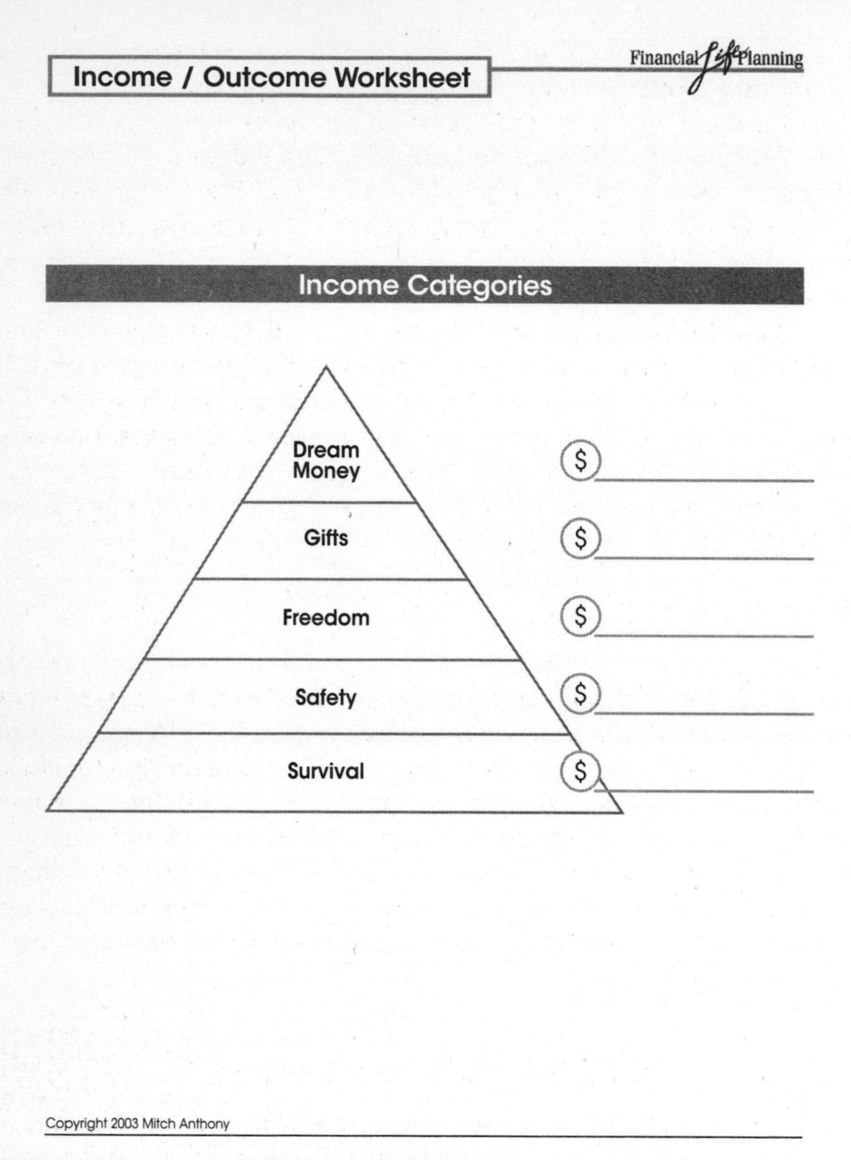

Figure 15.6 Income/Outcome Worksheet

within us. There will most likely be costs associated with planting that seed.

We dream of having and doing things. Maybe we want to have and do just for a while or maybe permanently, depending on whether we decide we like the having and being enough. But there are obvious costs to having (like owning a horse) and less obvious costs to doing (like owning the time needed to do what we will with it).

Owning one's own time is at the core of the need for self-actualization. How can we be and do what we dream of being and doing if our time is owned by another? Or consumed with simply paying bills? There are many in our culture whose dreams are drowning in inflated survival costs. They have some decisions to make.

There are many others who would be doing better economically if they pursued their heart's passion, but just don't realize it. (I've always been bothered by the assumption that if you follow your heart, you'll make less money.) If, however, you know what you really want to do will pay less, then a negotiation with your lifestyle will be necessary to get you to the position where you can begin collecting a "playcheck."

Paying for Your Life

Tally up your totals for each need on Maslow's hierarchy and you are now ready for working out the income side of your life ledger—how to pay for the life you need and want (see Figure 15.6). At some point, we all will need to engage in the process of figuring out how to make our income provide the lifestyle we want *and* last a lifetime. It is time to tie our assets to our liabilities. Financially speaking, all the totals you have factored into your Income for Life plan are financial liabilities. Peace of mind and contentment enter the picture when we designate exactly what assets will pay for which liabilities—and balance our lives.

Individual Retirement Attitude

- Take the time to calculate your bill for monthly survival.
- Know what the associated costs are for safety, freedom, love, and actualization to materialize in your life.
- Realize that life is not a dress rehearsal. Use what you have to live the best life you can.

CHAPTER 16

Don't Go It Alone

"The best interest of the patient is the only interest that matters."
—Dr. William Mayo

I have spent the better part of my life living in Rochester, Minnesota, the home of the world-renowned Mayo Clinic, an organization that has a well-earned reputation for excellence in health care. All of my children, at some point, have had surgeries there, and one observation my wife and I have made is how transparently sensitive and caring the practitioners have been. In a realm that is often populated by practitioners who can come off as detached and overly scientific in their approach, it is always a breath of fresh air to encounter a professional who truly seems to have your best interests at heart.

At the Mayo Clinic this is no accident of personality or culture. It is by design. Early in the development of the clinic, the Mayo brothers stated that the culture would be built upon three core principles: competence, caring, and integrity. Everyone in the organization, from the top of administration to those mopping the halls, is inculcated with these cultural principles of operation. I hope they can continue this culture in an age where quantity (seeing more patients) is more important than quality (spending more time with patients) in the health care realm.

I cite the Mayo example as an analogy to what we should expect to receive when we are seeking financial advice. After our health, our concern for our financial well-being occupies a high place on our totems of life. "Wealth care" ought to be approached with the same level of competence, caring, and integrity that has proven to produce great results in the realm of health care.

The temptation to put one's own interests ahead of those whom we ought to be serving can and does manifest in every realm, whether it be a doctor recommending a procedure, a mechanic recommending a repair, or a financial advisor recommending a fund. In every realm of practice we will find the Good, the Bad, and the Ugly. Many people have been financially harmed by incompetence, by a lack of concern and negligence, or by a lack of integrity in their financial matters, just like they may have been harmed by the same inadequacies in their health care pursuits or other matters of life.

If you have a bad experience with a doctor, do you neglect medical care? Think of your money management as fiscal health. For every selfishly motivated financial salesperson, there is a highly competent and personable professional out there who has built his reputation by helping others reach their goals by putting clients' interests first. We simply need to know how to distinguish one from the other. It can be easy to get fooled. In this chapter I want to make the case for finding someone who is competent, caring, and trustworthy for the very simple reason that saving yourself the stress is worth the price of oversight in the long run. Some of the reasons I think it is worth considering hiring a competent professional include:

1. We don't always know what we don't know.
2. We are tempted to follow the crowd.
3. Individual investors historically underperform the indexes (if you just parked your money over time).
4. It is time consuming and stressful to manage money on a day-to-day or week-to-week basis.

I Don't Always Know What I Don't Know

Remember the online brokerage ads and the do-it-yourself proponents who wanted you to believe that nobody is to be trusted and that you should do this all on your own? Call me stupid, but when I'm looking to blame someone for making the wrong financial moves, I find myself at the top of the list. I have made more than my share of mistakes—many of which would have been avoided with professional consultation. The opposite also holds true. There have been instances when my instincts were right and I allowed a professional to talk me out of a decision. But on the whole, I would rather find someone worthy of my trust and not have all the stress myself. In my case, I work with someone who advises *and* consults with me when I think I have an idea. The bottom line is that we need someone worthy of our trust.

We Are Tempted to Follow the Crowd

Bubbles happen in the markets because everyone is doing the same thing and it also happens to be the worst possible thing they could be doing at the time. The common thread through bubbles is greed, whether that greed is institutional or individual. The dot-com bubble happened because everyone thought the Nasdaq run would never end, while tech start-ups were burning cash like it was so much refuse. The reality check came with a thud. The housing bubble happened because people were cajoled into thinking their homes could only go up in value—and that, too, ended with an economy-shocking and recession-inducing thud.

Where are the masses rushing to next? Bonds? Risky income-producing investments? Take your guess. One thing you can be sure of is that human nature will not change: people will follow other people, and the majority will get burned. It's good to seek some contrarian advice now and then. We are emotionally driven creatures, and the recent findings in behavioral finance demonstrate that these emotions fool us and lead into poor financial decisions most of the time.

As with most things in life, you get what you pay for. That I can buy a stock for only $7 doesn't mean I'm going to profit from that purchase. In fact, because it is so easy and inexpensive to buy in and out of that stock, the odds are increased that I will act on impulse and trade in and out at the wrong times. *More important than the cost of making an investment is the quality of that investment.* You can easily go broke in a short time at $7 a trade. I'm reminded of a great Warren Buffett quip: "With enough insider information and a million dollars, you can go broke in a year."

Individual Investors Underperform

In 2012 Dalbar reported that although individual investors managed to keep up with the markets during that one year, over the long run (3, 5, and 20 years), they underperformed the markets.

The fact remains that having a trusted professional help you achieve your goals is well worth the expense. In another study focused on pension investments, trustee-managed accounts significantly outperformed individual investor accounts (15 percent versus 7.70 percent.)[1]

The self-directed, do-it-yourself approaches were motivated with good intentions, but most of us have neither the expertise nor the needed attention span to successfully manage such a proposition. When we look at the difference between returns on equity (12.9 percent) and doing it yourself (3.5 percent), most of us could have hired a negligent manager who charged 3 percent and did nothing but throw funds into stock indexes—and we would have done better. We would have suffered much less damage than what we did to ourselves with ill-timed moves and very bad Warren Buffett imitations.[2]

The point is to have as much money as possible available for you to do with what you want. We can be our own worst enemy when it comes to reaching this point. Know your ability, availability, and attention span, do what is best for you in the long run, and make sure you get help where you need it.

Managing Money Is Time Consuming and Stressful

I see many folks who are what I would call "hobbyists" with their money—they devote a great deal of time to market news, stock and fund prices, and the latest breathless headlines on CNBC. However, I rarely see such a hobbyist who is not fairly high strung and experiencing manic periods of financial stress. I have often joked with the do-it-myself crowd that their first investment should be in Procter & Gamble, the maker of Pepto-Bismol, because their consumption will surely be going up. There will always be stress around financial decision making, but you need to choose between the stress of finding the right advice or the stress of advising yourself on a day-to-day basis.

Some people manage their own stock and/or mutual fund portfolios and get decent returns. Some of these people are truly savvy investors, and others are fortunate beneficiaries of a bull market (or they simply are missing bear markets) and good timing. The more your portfolio grows, the more you may feel the need to get some help in making the right financial decisions. Many people seem quite content to remain alone while *growing* their assets, but that mind-set is subject to change when the issue shifts to *protecting* those assets.

Ask yourself these two questions:

1. Do I know everything I need to know about asset allocation and protection, tax-reduction strategies, and estate management?
2. Do I want to invest the time and effort to learn these issues? Do I want to continue to invest the time it takes to keep up with the markets and remain competent as an investor?

If you answered yes to these questions and have the time and interest in devoting yourself to building and protecting your assets, then you can go it alone. One caveat: don't assume you can possibly know all there is to know. Even if you want to do it on your own, it would be wise to pay for a consultation and get some direction from a professional money manager who knows her way around the brambles of managing risk, tax consequences, and more. Some professionals consult for an hourly fee or for a one-time fee.

If you know exactly what you want to own (stocks, bonds, mutual funds, etc.), know how to go about buying those holdings at the best price, and are not bothered by the stress of keeping up, then you may be a candidate to do it on your own. This assumes that you are well informed and can keep up on those holdings for any changes that could threaten the security of your investments.

Finding a Wealth-Building Partner

Because of the nature of my work, I have met literally thousands of brokers, advisors, planners, bankers, and accountants. All of these professionals are clamoring for your business. Some of these professionals I would trust my financial life to because of their integrity and competence. Others I wouldn't give a wooden nickel to because of their self-centeredness and lack of competence. Some of them are so busy selling that they don't really keep up with the products they are supposed to be expert in. They just keep telling the same story and selling the same products to everyone. Others I have met listen with great curiosity to each of their clients to figure out a strategy that is best for their clients, and then work hard to earn the clients' trust and loyalty.

Maybe you have heard or read stories or have had a bad experience yourself with a self-serving broker or advisor. "Once burned, their fault; twice burned, my fault," you tell yourself. There are some bad apples (read selfish) and some good apples out there. You need to establish a clear profile of the type of person you want to work with and start interviewing until you find a match that feels right to you. Finding a match is as much about personal chemistry as it is financial philosophy.

After observing this wide range of integrity/competence, I have developed the following criteria for interviewing a financial professional. Use this assessment after talking to a professional, and you will greatly increase your odds of finding the wealth-building partner you need.

1. *What was your first impression of the individual?* Was she personable and respectful, or officious, self-absorbed, overly saccharine-coated, or arrogant?

   The individual's personality is a good indicator of the kind of service and attention you can expect to receive down the road should problems or concerns arise.
2. *What kind of questions did the financial professional ask you?* Did he ask more about your money and the size of your portfolio or more about your life scenarios, financial experiences, and goals?
3. *Did the financial professional demonstrate good listening skills?* Did she carefully summarize your concerns, goals, and level of risk tolerance?

   If you get the feeling you are not dealing with a good listener, move on. If the individual is paying close attention now, you know that is what you can expect later. If the individual pretends to listen but just charges ahead with an agenda that seems to miss the point of what you told her, move on. If the professional dominates the conversation, get out as fast as you can!
4. *Did the financial professional explain matters in a language you could understand, or did he use jargon and talk over your head?*

   Those who talk over your head probably want to keep you in the dark or simply aren't smart enough to make matters understandable. Anyone who makes you feel stupid is not worthy of your business. A sure sign of competence is the ability to make complex matters seem simple and understandable. A good advisor will also be a good teacher and will help you improve your financial well-being. A good advisor isn't afraid of having a smart client!

5. *Is the financial professional willing to disclose her own personal holdings?*

   You would be amazed at the number of financial professionals whose personal financial lives are in disarray. There are also many who are not buying what they are selling. If financial professionals are trying to sell something they don't own, I want to know why. If you find an advisor who does for her clients what she does for herself, you have a greater potential for trust.

6. *Does the financial professional have a track record that can be documented?*

   Unless you want to be somebody's guinea pig, you should ask to see the professional's performance record. Check to see that the individual has done well in down markets as well as in up markets. Ask for references and talk to those who have been clients for a long period. You can conduct a background check on an advisor at finra.org (www.finra.org/Investors/ToolsCalculators/BrokerCheck/).

7. *Does the financial professional articulate a clear philosophy regarding investments and wealth building?*

   If the professional doesn't have a clear philosophical compass that has been fine-tuned through experience, he is more likely to be one of those individuals who follows the crowd or the firm's latest recommendation. The dime-a-dozen advisor who sells whatever he is told to sell is not the person you are looking for. I like to see advisors who are comfortable talking about their mistakes as well as their victories—a good investment philosophy borrows from the lessons of both failure and success.

8. *Ask the financial professional how and why she got into this business.*

   Here, you will hear answers ranging from seemingly being on a mission to help other people to seemingly only pretending to be on a mission to help other people but are really on a mission to help themselves. I read between the lines on this answer. I want to get the sense that the financial professional is fascinated about money matters, curious about people, and motivated by her work.

If you walk out of an interview satisfied that these bases have been covered, you have a greater chance of partnering with a trustworthy individual. Cunning individuals may have the ability to fake these integral characteristics, but they cannot fake them for long. You want a concerned and competent professional who is in the profession for the right reasons. You want to find out what the person's motives are. After taking him or her through the preceding questions, you will have a fairly good indication.

A Personal Safety Net

When I was building an addition onto my home for our new baby boy, I decided I wanted to do some of the work myself to save money. I had a little experience doing electrical wiring and decided to tackle it with a little consultation. The builder agreed to inspect my work before the official inspector came in. When I was done with the wiring, the builder came to check my work. When he came to the last connection I had made, he showed me how I had erred and informed me that it could have easily started a fire. Then and there I decided some projects are far too important to try to tackle alone with a limited degree of experience. I believe that retirement or emancipation planning is one of those projects.

Even with the wealth of free online information available, when I travel to a faraway place I like to get the advice of a trusted travel agent who has actually been there. I have found that faraway places don't always look and feel as pleasant as they appear in the brochure pictures. Sure, I pay more by not doing it on my own, but my travel agent provides me with two intangibles that I value: experience and confidence. I want the peace of mind that comes from knowing I will not have unpleasant surprises when I arrive. I think of a good financial professional as a tour guide in a fiscal maze.

Guides of every description can be found today: advisors who charge a one-time fee to design an investment plan; advisors who charge consultation fees by the hour; advisors who charge a small percentage of assets under management (they make more money when you make more money). You can find a person and an arrangement you will be comfortable with in today's financial marketplace. Good financial professionals are worth their weight in gold. For example, Janet Briaud, a financial advisor in Texas, makes sure there's a fit before she takes on a new client (regardless of the amount of assets they may be investing with her):

> New clients have at least two meetings with Briaud before any planning is done. The first is a let's-get-acquainted-and-learn-to-trust-each-other session that Briaud describes as "rather touchy-feely." If she and the client do not hit it off, or if she senses that the person is unwilling to make a long-term commitment, that individual will be referred elsewhere. Indeed, one prospect was rejected because he was surly and condescending to the office staff. (He later apologized, got a second chance, and turned into a model client.)
>
> If all goes well at the introduction, Briaud schedules a goal-setting meeting, which she considers the most important work she does for clients. This session lasts at least two hours and often much longer.[3]

You have a greater chance of reaching your emancipation goals with guidance, accountability, and coaching. A good advisor will provide you with all of these. It simply comes down to finding someone you can trust—someone who wants the satisfaction of helping you reach your goals.

Individual Retirement Attitude

The individual retirement attitude recognizes both the freedoms and perils of the new financial marketplace, and recognizes the need for wisdom and experience, not just information and the lowest fee. The individual retirement attitude recognizes that if people want to, they can do the work and go it alone; but it also recognizes the value of the time and stress that can be saved by joining up with the right wealth-building partner.

From Aging to S-Aging

"I think 65 is a phony age. I don't see why we should be losing the productivity of people at a certain age. There is very little reason why there should be an artificial age limitation at all."

—Elinor Guggenheimer, author

I often ask audiences if they know someone who is 75 years old and acts like he is 35 and see appreciative nods. I then ask if they know someone who is 45 who acts like she is 80 and see the eyes roll and the knowing nods. The question I then like to pose is this: what, then, are we saying about one's "real age" and the aging process? We are assenting to the idea that, though one's age is a matter of chronology, aging itself is largely a matter of attitude. There can be a wide disparity between being a certain age and acting out that age—hence the phrase "you're as young as you think." The fact that we know 75-year-olds who act 45 affirms the attitudinal and spiritual source of that which separates those who are aging from those who are old.

Old isn't what it used to be. Remember that when the age for retirement was originally set at 65, a majority of people didn't even live until retirement age. Now we live 20 to 30 years past the retirement age. The age of 65 in this day and age has little resemblance to the age of 65 in, say, 1980. Most people are not old at 65 today. They may or may not have slowed down. Thirty years ago you didn't see many men in their 70s and 80s jumping out of airplanes, flying in outer space, or riding skateboards. You may recall the story I shared earlier about the four generations of family water skiing in synchronicity: great grandpa at 92, grandpa at 63, dad at 40, and junior at 5! These types of activity will serve as portents of the active lifestyles in seniors of the future. We will see more and more of the aging role models in years to come.

It is ironic that our society, rather than adjusting to this longevity trend, continues to promote a retirement age that was established over 125 years ago. Many have failed to comprehend that if they retire at 60, for example, they could spend as many years in their retirement as they did in their working career. This is great if you have some invigorating and challenging pursuits before you in those 30+ years. If you don't, history shows that you'll never see those 30 extra years.

How old will you be when you really become old? It seems that the answer to that question is as individual as the person answering it. We know that the marker for old is no longer 65. Some recent surveys show that most seniors now feel that the marker for old is somewhere nearer 80. Expect that number to keep moving up with the Baby Boom generation.

> *"While one finds company in himself and his pursuits, he cannot feel old, no matter what his years may be."*
>
> —Amos Alcott

Most people feel that "old" is defined by a decline in mental or physical abilities, while less than half feel it is defined by age. Years ago, author Dr. Michael F. Roizen wrote a *New York Times* bestseller entitled *Real Age* that enlarged on this idea of locating each individual's "real age," which is the true reflection of one's physical and mental state.[1] After poring over 25,000 medical studies, Roizen and his associates came to the conclusion that age is much more than a chronological marker. Dr. Roizen presents physical, mental, and lifestyle criteria by which each individual can gauge his or her own aging process. In fact, Roizen and his associates came up with over 100 different health behaviors, ranging from diet to stress control, that enable you to assess your real age. More than a chronological marker, age is really the rate at which your internal guardians of health—cardiovascular and immune systems—decline. There is much we can do to slow that decline.

Roizen's book and web site (realage.com) offers a "real age" test that you can take to see how old you really are. This test covers a broad range of health factors, including habits and conditions (smoking, sex, diet, exercise, driving, drinking, prescription drugs, exposure to dangerous activities), nutritional intake, weight, health history, family genes, stress, social connections, and relaxation practices. After this assessment, Roizen challenges readers to develop an age reduction program. He provides evidence that such a program helps you live and feel up to 26 years younger—many physical, mental, and spiritual practices can add years to our lives.

A Sense of Mastery

A MacArthur Foundation study on aging, featured in the book *Successful Aging*, described how one ages successfully. It used the phrase "a sense of mastery" to describe how individuals must believe in their ability to influence events and control their outcomes to be positive and productive in their later years. They found that during a period of less than three years, those who increased their sense of mastery also increased their productivity. The opposite also held true—those whose sense of personal mastery decreased saw a significant reduction in their involvement in productive activities.[2] What exactly is personal mastery? It is self-reliance.

What exactly does it take to become more self-reliant and shift your life into a higher state of confidence and healthy, active living? Three important factors come into play:

1. An opportunity to undertake a specific action that challenges one's sense of self-sufficiency without overwhelming it.
2. The presence of supporting and reassuring others.
3. The experience of succeeding at something with confirming feedback from others.

A sense of confidence works on the same dynamics at any age. We imagine ourselves doing something. We muster the courage and abandon our inhibitions to try it. We look for feedback for our efforts from the people around us. A historical pitfall of aging is the narrowed radius of the comfort zones that can control a person at age 65. "I've never done that," "I don't know anything about computers," and "I'm too old to start that now" are examples of verbal indicators that the fossilizing process is already under way. The fact that you often hear 50-year-old people making such statements is proof that "old" can start at any age.

The MacArthur Foundation study concluded that the three indicators of successful aging are:

1. Avoiding disease and disability.
2. Maintaining mental and physical function.
3. Continuing engagement with life.

More than 10 years later, the findings of this landmark study still apply. Many factors come into play in order to age successfully. The physical, intellectual, social, and spiritual aspects of our being must be attended to equally if we hope to hold back the hands of time. We can readily observe the effect of not attending to one or more of these areas in the lives of people we know who practiced such negligence. It does not take long for the aging process to kick into high gear if we let down our guards of discipline and purposefulness.

The first key to aging successfully is to take an interest in yourself. It doesn't take long in the company of elderly people to figure out which ones are feeling sorry for themselves and which ones are extracting every ounce of life's possibilities. Those who succeed are self-respecting enough to keep their bodies fit, their minds challenged, and their hearts engaged.

Figure out how old you *truly* are in mind and body, and introduce yourself to people who are defying the so-called limitations of age. These individuals have not bought into the idea that they need to move aside for the next generation—or anyone else for that matter. They will leave the race when they are good and ready.

The Vitamin Cs of Successful Aging

Aging reflects the relationship of time on our being. Aging describes, in large part, the state of our body. *Old,* however, describes our state of mind. It has always been a matter of great interest to me to discover the spiritual and attitudinal aquifer that supplies the fountain of youth.

There is no denying the effects of time on our bodies. Although we can slow certain physical impacts, we cannot prevent them altogether. Hair turns gray or falls out. Skin wrinkles. Senses like hearing and sight can begin to dull—as can short-term memory function. As George Burns once quipped: "You know you're getting older when everything hurts, and what doesn't hurt doesn't work."

> *"Though our outward man perishes, our inward man is renewed day by day."*
>
> —The Apostle Paul's letter to Corinth

Equally immutable as the decaying dynamic of physical being is the constantly renewing and refreshing dynamic of our inner being. This dynamic of engaged living until the day we die is not automatic but is accomplished by the purposeful and intentional discipline of those souls who choose to *live* every day. They accept the inevitability of death, but simply have chosen not to give death a head start in their souls. Attitude becomes a matter of preeminence, for attitude is the rudder that steers the ship on this journey.

Release the rudder for a single day and you can sense a sort of existential seasickness. Release it for a week, and you will drift aimlessly or be tossed on the rocks. Release the rudder for any longer period and shipwreck is inevitable. This is a truth I have witnessed time and again on the retirement landscape.

So, in observing the forever young, forever passionate, and forever engaged, I have come across five internal focuses and patterns constituting what I refer to as *the attitude instrument*—that which steers our lives safely through the existential seas of fulfilled and pleasurable living day by day. I call these focuses the Vitamin Cs of successful aging:

- Vitamin C1—Connectivity
- Vitamin C2—Challenge
- Vitamin C3—Curiosity
- Vitamin C4—Creativity
- Vitamin C5—Charity

Vitamin C1—Connectivity

A study conducted at the University of Michigan found that in retirement, psychological well-being increases for some individuals and decreases for others. The researchers analyzed variables of physical health, income level, traumatic life experiences in recent years, age, gender, and other factors that might affect the psychological well-being of an individual. They found that the most powerful predictor of life satisfaction right after retirement was not health or wealth but the breadth of a person's social network.[3]

Why do people retire and immediately move away to a place where they have no social connectivity? Not only are they disconnecting from a major lifeline in the science of successful aging, they might also find out they are annoyed with the accents and culture into which they moved. It might be wise to spend some time doing reconnaissance on the geography and culture where you plan on staging the next act of your life. Many people disconnect themselves from important social networks when they retire and don't realize it until it's too late.

Stay connected to people you love, people you enjoy, and people who appreciate you and see value in your presence. Longevity does not favor the Lone Ranger. Both long life and happiness are tied to the quality of your connections.

Vitamin C2—Challenge

The latest Alzheimer's research demonstrates that being intellectually challenged and having predictable taxation on our mental acuity literally have the effect of a finger in the dike, holding back the degenerative processes leading to both Alzheimer's and dementia. This research also concluded that as we hit our 50s and beyond, there is an exigency on ensuring that we have riddles to ponder, problems to solve, and things to fix. The brain is a muscle that atrophies without use. One gentleman told me that after six months of retirement, he could literally sense the dulling in his cerebral muscle with signs of slowed thinking and sluggish articulation.

> *"I decided to go back to college part-time when I reached age 62 and study psychology for no other reason than that I was curious about it. I've always wanted to get a better understanding of human behavior and I figured this was one step toward getting it. When I started classes, I was amazed at how many people were there in my age group. I guess I'm not the only curious grandma out there. I spent my career in business management. I got my fill of that. Now I feel like I'm in the middle of an electric storm. My mind is on full alert. I'm in awe of some of the things I'm learning. I have these*

intriguing conversations with younger people and just doing this makes me feel like I can go anywhere and do anything."

—Georgia, student

The pulsating vein of life that Georgia has tapped into, along with a growing contingent of mature citizens, is growth. I hold little hope for the aging individuals who live with the delusion that they have "seen and heard it all." Those who have curiosity racing through their brains are guaranteed an exciting existence. Curiosity fuels both optimism and hope. Lifetime learners have the attitude that their quality of life will rise with their application to learning. This older entrance into new realms of education is, and will continue to be, a growing trend with the end of retirement as we know it. More and more retirees are moving to university towns instead of retirement villages.

It is important to note here that a job of some sort may be the most important source for cognitive demands because it is a primary source of mental stimulation. In *Successful Aging*, authors John W. Rowe and Robert L. Kahn wrote: "Remember the old adage, 'We become what we do'? People whose jobs promote self-direction, use of initiative, and independent judgment tend to boost their intellectual flexibility—that is, their ability to use a variety of approaches in order to solve mental problems." In short, mental flexibility is as important as intellectual curiosity as we age, and being active in challenging work can nurture such mental elasticity. An old and changing stereotype of aging is the old man or woman who won't listen to new ideas. Mental curiosity and flexibility are the answer to that old problem.

Vitamin C3—Curiosity

On a flight home from Australia, I sat next to Ken Clark, a physicist from the University of Washington. At that time he was in his late 70s, still teaching and researching. I asked him why he wasn't retired, as was expected of a man his age. His answer was, "There's so much yet to learn," and he enthusiastically began describing his latest upper atmospheric physics research project. When I saw the sparkle in Dr. Clark's eyes as he spoke, I realized how good it would be if more seniors had their heads in the clouds of higher learning. Curiosity guarantees a pulse in the brain and a reason to keep our bodies healthy. The role of mental alertness cannot be overestimated, and neither can the benefits of a desire to grow. Once a person reaches a point where he no longer wants to learn or grow, it is time to order the tombstone. It need not be formal education that we pursue; it can be self-taught or experiential learning. The important thing is to have the curiosity and desire to grow. Age is an uphill road. Learning and tasks that demand mental alertness keep us in gear. Those of us who stay neutral in this area will quickly find we are going backward. Rigorous mental function helps to both facilitate productivity in later years and strengthen our need and desire to be active—factors that in turn affect our physical well-being.

Vitamin C4—Creativity

I've long been enthralled by elderly artists in their 80s and 90s who seem as keen and perspicacious as people half their age. I once listened to an interview with a Canadian artist in her 90s, whose lucidity of thought and spry articulation was inspiring. She also confirmed my suspicions about the virtues of creative engagement in our later years. She talked about the aforementioned curiosity being razor-sharp as well. She reasoned that artists have developed a *discipline of observation* that requires seeing what others who are less curious, might miss. A creative soul looks at the shoreline and sees something new every day. This might help explain why B. B. King, over 80, is still going strong, and why Peter Drucker was able to write a business bestseller in his 90s. Of course, you don't have to be renowned to be creative and to keep the powers of observation working. You just have to be curious, intrigued, expressive, and intentional. A couple of other gems I heard this elderly artist mention were regularly scheduled, intellectually stimulating luncheons with people younger than herself; a profoundly diminished sense of self-consciousness; and two ounces of Canadian rye whiskey each evening for good measure.

Vitamin C5—Charity

Studies continue to surface around the ameliorative effects of charitable living on quality and longevity of life. Those who think about helping others often talk about how such charitable preoccupations lessen the degenerative effects of stress associated with worrying. Even if we didn't live a day longer because of charitable pursuits, we no doubt would live better.

Remember the story in Chapter 15 about financial planner Roy Diliberto's client? Her life completely turned around after he challenged her to look around her city for places she might like to make a difference. Her gift to others was also a gift to herself. Remember, it doesn't require money to live charitably; it just takes concern, generosity, and self-transcendence.

Pumping Iron at 80

On a recent summer vacation, I ended up playing golf with Don. I complimented his tee shot, which went about 180 yards right down the middle of the fairway. His response was, "Well, I'm starting to gain a little distance back with my upper body training. But that one there isn't too bad for an 80-year-old man, wouldn't you say?" At first look, you would guess Don to be around 70. I was amused by the irony of Don's telling me that he was gaining yardage on his drives. I have hardly ever played golf with a person over 60 who, at some point in the round, would not begin lamenting the loss of yardage that comes with gaining of years. Yet here was Don talking about a strength-training program he had just begun at age 80! He also told me that he played 18 holes a day as well as walking the two miles to and from the golf course each day.

According to various studies and the American Psychological Association, exercise and physical activity is directly related to successful aging.[4] In fact, physical *inactivity* is a predictor of things to come: increased falls, fractures, heart disease, respiratory disease, diabetes, and more! It's not a pretty picture. A more specific point to consider is that muscle mass declines by 1 to 2 percent a year past the age of 50 (if we're not addressing the matter) and this affects our strength, our endurance, and our balance. That fact alone should be enough to get all of us pumping some iron on a weekly basis. Not only will you feel better, this type of exercise has been shown to improve cognitive ability as well (so you'll not only know when someone is insulting you, you'll be able to flex your bicep to stop them).

> *"Much of what we think of as aging is really just a by-product of inactivity and poor nutrition, and it's not hard to change that."*
>
> —Miriam Nelson, physiologist,
> USDA Research Center on Aging

The MacArthur study on aging referenced earlier found that older people who engaged in strenuous physical activity at home were more likely to maintain their high cognitive function. A cyclical relationship exists between body, mind, and spirit. It is difficult at times to explain, but, once experienced, it is well understood. According to various studies reported on in *Translational Psychiatry*, cognitive function definitely improves with exercise.[5] Results indicated that higher levels of physical exercise were associated with better cognitive performance. According to an article in *JAMA*, the apparent cognitive benefits of exercise compare with "being about three years younger." Once lethargy infects a person's body, it seems that within a short time it invades the mind and spirit as well. Soon energy levels are lower, the mind is less perspicacious, and optimism is affected as well. We cannot wait to feel energy to become fit. We foster a discipline of fitness in order to gain energy. The action precedes the feeling. Positive physical regimens like walking (those who walk just three to five miles a week add five or more years to their life span), weight lifting, dietary discipline, and regular physical checkups all add years to the life span. Just as important, these regimens add quality to the years we live. Why live to be 90 if we're going to drag through 30 of those years with low energy and waning enthusiasm? Use your mind, engage your body, and nurture your spirit.

The Soul of Accelerated Aging

I have probably learned the most about how I will approach aging from the contrast between my two grandmas' lifestyles and attitudes. Both of my grandmas are well into their 80s, but their life contentment factors are like night and day. One is always playing the martyr, poor-little-me game every time any of us talk to her. Until recently, she has been in pretty good health, but she would exaggerate any symptoms into life-threatening stories to get attention. She has isolated herself socially. When I ask her if she has met any new friends, she says that she is too old to make any new friends. When we visit her, she complains about how short our stay is and tries to manipulate us into staying longer. I hate to say it, but when I think of her, I often think of complaining, whining, and self-centeredness.

My other grandma, on the other hand, though handicapped in both sight and mobility, is active, positive, and socially engaged. She is active in the senior citizen's center, volunteers as a peer mentor in an Alzheimer's support group (having lost her husband to that disease), has regular conversations, participates in games and activities—which fills her schedule each day. She loves to talk about the things she is involved in and is looking forward to. She also enjoys meeting new people. To me, her most outstanding attribute is her sense of gratitude. She seems to relish each day and each moment. When I visit with her, she's thankful for the time and conversation, even if it's just a few moments. Rarely do you hear a complaint even though she could list a litany of very real problems. She is a joy to others, and many people look forward to seeing her each day even though as she says, 'They look forward to seeing me and I look forward to hearing them.'

The irony of this tale of two grandmothers is that they both have lived long lives so far. But that is where the similarity ends. I want meaningful longevity in my life, not prolonged existence. Living to 90 for one person is a blessing and to another an oxymoron. In my opinion, self-absorption seems to be at the seat of miserable aging.

—Ann, 45

Research from the Cornell study on retirement and well-being indicates that those who give of themselves boost their self-esteem and also gain a sense of more control over their own life.[6] Researchers studied both workers and retirees between the ages of 50 and 72 and came to this conclusion: "Community commitments, especially formal participation, help enhance our sense of identity, promote ongoing networks of social relationships, and foster expectations of what to do when we wake up in the morning." There is an observable difference in the aging of the soul between the self-absorbed person and the selfless one. Giving to others, volunteering, and being a part of meaningful, significant activities seem to help promote healthier attitudes, which in turn improve one's health and contentment in life.

John Rowe and Robert Kahn tell the story of Phyllis, who remained productive and engaged in spite of her many functional limitations and chronic diseases. Phyllis, at 80, continued her work as an actress despite three heart attacks, major heart surgery, colon cancer, and a serious fall that led to lung failure and more heart problems. She continues to perform on stage at least two to three months a year. When not acting in a show, she volunteers in the theater world by serving at the box office, doing mailings, and the like. She is also an avid theatergoer as well. Phyllis articulated her secret for being able to move forward and remain productive this way: "Keep your interest in outer things, not inner ones. Keep busy. And always maintain more interests than there is time for."

In the old Greek myth of Narcissus, the man consumed with his own image, eventually dies of starvation because he cannot stand to leave the pool of water where he beholds his own image. We use the term *narcissism* to describe individuals who are consumed with themselves. In the study of successful aging, a lesson seems to appear later in life, this time as a wrinkled Narcissus beholding his image in the same pool of water. But instead of being enamored with himself, he becomes self-pitying at the sight of his decline and appearance. He wallows in so much self-pity that he will not leave to do anything to reverse his decline.

Americans generally feel that retirees have too little influence in the country today. This will change as new retirees keep their connections alive, remain relevant, redefine the life stage, and work toward impacting their communities, workplaces, and societies.

The New Retirementality has no time for a self-pitying stare into our aging image. We must follow the ageless image we have within us—and stay connected to this world.

Individual Retirement Attitude

- Continue your education and mental challenge throughout life.
- Maintain a positive social network of friends and associates throughout life-stage changes.
- Look for ways to stay engaged and make a contribution in your mature years.

Appendix

RETIRING ON PURPOSE: A CONVERSATION ABOUT MAKING THIS THE MOST MEANINGFUL STAGE OF LIFE YET

Retiring with a Purpose

"I have seen far too many retirees adrift on a sea of aimlessness, boredom, and discontentment. They found their freedom from the old job and the old routines but didn't sufficiently contemplate what that freedom could lead them toward.

"There is an entire generation of people arising who have decided to make the "third age" of life the most meaningful. This group understands the habits, attitudes, and pursuits that directly correlate with successful aging and staying young at heart. Words like curiosity, connectivity, challenge, and contributing are hallmarks of a new generation of retirees, who are transforming 'retiring' into 'refiring' and 'reclining' into 'refining.' These people are leaving an indelible impact on the people, the ideas, and the causes they care most about."

—Mitch Anthony

Retirement Reflections

Observations I have made and lessons I have learned from watching others retire:

____

____

____

____

___

___

The Transcendent Life

JOB: Something I have to do
INTEREST: Something I enjoy doing
MISSION: My reason for being

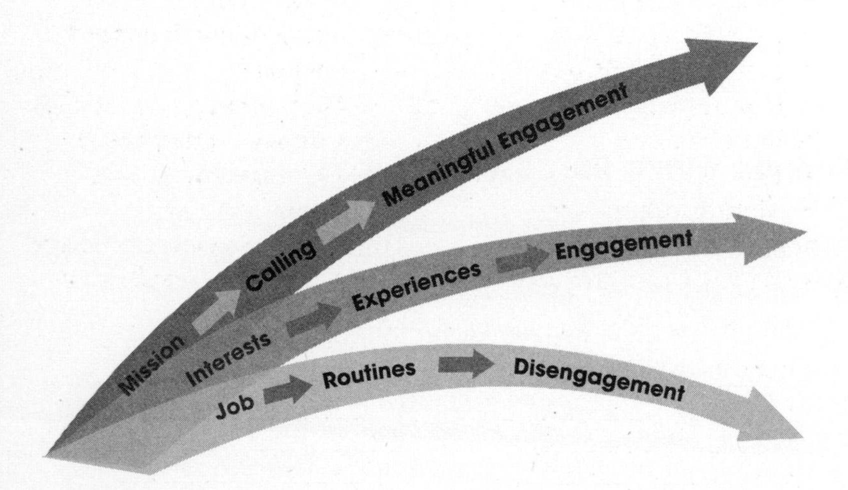

Our quality of life depends largely on our quality of engagement. Working a job we don't particularly enjoy leads to routinous living and a disengaged spirit. Pursuing interests we enjoy causes us to look forward to the experience—and we are engaged in the process. The highest level of living is engaging in mission (something we feel called to do), which is tied to calling (something we feel we must accomplish), which in turn fuels a sense of purposeful engagement—our reason for being.

For Everything There Is a Season

Select five choices from the list below that best describe your next phase of life and place on your (A) list. Place your second five choices on the (B) list.

I see retirement as a time to:

- Travel
- Relax
- Teach others
- Spend time with spouse
- Explore
- Learn new skills
- Connect with family
- Engage in a hobby
- Do projects at home
- Start a new business
- Continue present work
- Find balance
- Play
- Mentor others
- Connect with friends
- Educate myself
- Work with charities
- Help out with kids
- Take it easy
- Go back to school
- Dust off old dreams
- Do consulting work
- Increase my community involvement
- Hang out with retired friends
- Help others
- Connect with a cause
- Get a part-time hobby job
- Take on a new challenge
- Write about experiences

A List	B List
• ____________	• ____________
• ____________	• ____________
• ____________	• ____________
• ____________	• ____________
• ____________	• ____________

"There is a big difference between 'having made it' and 'having it made.'"

—Mitch Anthony

Purposeful Retirement

Connecting with Others—Who I desire to build stronger connections with, and why:

1. ____________________
2. ____________________
3. ____________________

Challenging Myself*—How I will continue to challenge my intellect, my faculties, and my will:

1. ______________________________
2. ______________________________
3. ______________________________

Contributing to Others—People and causes I would like to assist:

1. ______________________________
2. ______________________________
3. ______________________________

Exploration Agenda

Places I would like to go:

1. ______________________________
2. ______________________________
3. ______________________________

Experiences I would like to try:

1. ______________________________
2. ______________________________
3. ______________________________

Skills I'd like to learn:

1. ______________________________
2. ______________________________
3. ______________________________

People I'd like to meet:

1. ______________________________
2. ______________________________
3. ______________________________

---

*Studies demonstrate that conditions like Alzheimer's disease and dementia are accelerated without continued intellectual challenge from one's 40s onward.

> *"Having exciting agendas on the horizon infuses people with hope and a joy of living."*
>
> —Mitch Anthony

Mission Accomplished

Place yourself 30 years down the road and you are looking back on your accomplishments. What goals and objectives do you hope to have accomplished in these three decades?

For Myself:

____

____

____

For Others:

____

____

____

Notes

Chapter 1

1. Laura Davidow Hirshbein, "William Osler and the Fixed Period: Conflicting Medical and Popular Ideas About Old Age," *Archives of Internal Medicine* 161, no. 17 (2001): 2074–78. http://deepblue.lib.umich.edu/bitstream/handle/2027.42/83267/LDH%20Osler.pdf;jsessionid=2877C7F3D76B01A8F96F1453D241BD86?sequence=1.
2. Dora L. Costa, "The Evolution of Retirement." In *The Evolution of Retirements: An American Economic History, 1880–1990,* edited by Dora L. Costa (Chicago: University of Chicago Press, 1998). www.nber.org/chapters/c6108.pdf.
3. "Life Expectancy for Social Security." Social Security Administration. www.socialsecurity.gov/history/lifeexpect.html.

Chapter 2

1. Matt Sedensky, "Could Phased Retirement Work for You?" *AARP Blog,* May 30, 2012. http://blog.aarp.org/2013/05/30/phased-retirement-helps-older-workers-transition-into-retired-life/.
2. Ruth Helman, Craig Copeland, and Jack VanDerhei, "2012 Retirement Confidence Survey: Job Insecurity, Debt Weigh on Retirement Confidence, Savings," EBRI Issue Brief no. 369, March 2012.
3. Insured Retirement Institute, "Boomer Expectations for Retirement 2012: Annual Update on Retirement Preparedness of the Boomer Generation," April 2012.

Chapter 3

1. Barbara Griffina, Beryl Hesketh, and Vanessa Lohaa, "The Influence of Subjective Life Expectancy on Retirement Transition and Planning: A Longitudinal Study," *Journal of Vocational Behavior* 81, no. 2 (October 2012): 129–37. http://dx.doi.org/10.1016/j.jvb.2012.05.005.
2. Hanna van Solinge and Kène Henkens, "Living Longer, Working Longer? The Impact of Subjective Life Expectancy on Retirement Intentions and Behaviour." *European Journal of Public Health* 20, no. 1 (October 12, 2009): 47–51. http://eurpub.oxfordjournals.org/content/20/1/47.abstract?sid=1510875d-0fc7-42f5-9482-e32c28790c2e.

3. M. E. von Bonsdorff, K. S. Shultz, E. Leskinen, & J. Tansky, "The Choice between Retirement and Bridge Employment: A Continuity Theory and Life Course Perspective." *International Journal of Aging and Human Devleopment* 69 (2009): 79–100.
4. B. Hesketh, B. Griffin, and V. Loh, "A Future-Oriented Retirement Transition Adjustment Framework." *Journal of Vocational Behavior* 12 (2009).
5. "Aegon Retirement Readiness Survey 2012: The Changing Face of Retirement." www.aegon.com/Documents/aegon-com/Sitewide/Retirement-Readiness-Survey/The-Changing-Face-of-Retirement-The-Workplace-Perspective.pdf?epslanguage=en.

Chapter 4

1. National Endowment for Financial Education, "Retirement Planning in the 21st Century," May 26–28, 1999. www.nefe.org/Portals/0/WhatWeProvide/PrimaryResearch/PDF/RetirementPlanninginthe21stCentury_May99.pdf.

Chapter 5

1. Gabriel H. Sahlgren, "Work Longer, Live Healthier: The Relationship between Economic Activity, Health and Government Policy." IEA Discussion Paper no. 46, May 2013. www.iea.org.uk/sites/default/files/in-the-media/files/Work%20Longer,%20Live_Healthier.pdf.
2. Shan P. Tsai, Judy K. Wendt, Robin P. Donnelly, Geert de Jong, and Farah S. Ahmed, "Age at Retirement and Long Term Survival of an Industrial Population: Prospective Cohort Study." *BMJ* 331 (2005): 995. www.bmj.com/content/331/7523/995.
3. Steve Vernon, "Does Working Longer Increase Your Lifespan?" CBSNews.com, March 8, 2010. www.cbsnews.com/8301-505146_162-39940199/does-working-longer-increase-your-lifespan/.
4. S. L. Brown and I. F. Lin, "The Gray Divorce Revolution: Rising Divorce among Middle-Aged and Older Adults, 1990–2010." *Journals of Gerontology Series B: Psychological Sciences and Social Sciences,* 67, no. 6 (October 9, 2012): 731–41, doi:10.1093/geronb/gbs089.
5. B. Ashforth, *Role Transitions in Organizational Life: An Identity-Based Perspective* (Mahwah, NJ: Lawrence Erlbaum, 2001).
6. M. Wang and K. S. Schultz, "Employee Retirement: A Review and Recommendations for Future Investigation," *Journal of Management* 36 (2010): 172–206.
7. K. Henkens, H. van Solinge, and W. T. Gallo, W. T., "Effects of Retirement Voluntariness on Changes in Smoking, Drinking and Physical Activity among Dutch Older Workers," *European Journal of Public Health* 18 (2008): 644–49.

Chapter 6

1. Transamerica Center for Retirement Studies. "13th Annual Retirement Study," 2012. www.transamericacenter.org/resources/tc_center_research.html.

2. Tamara Lytle, "Are You Planning on Working into Your Retirement Years?" *AARP Blog,* May 24, 2013. http://blog.aarp.org/2013/05/24/working-past-retirement-age-retiring-later-in-life-building-nest-egg/print/.
3. Insured Retirement Institute, "Boomer Expectations for Retirement 2012," April 2012.
4. BAI and Financial Research Corporation, "2009 Retirement Study: Capitalize on Market Opportunities," October 2009. www.frcnet.com/documents/2009-BAI-FRC-Retirement-Study-Fact-Sheet.pdf.

Chapter 7

1. Ruth Helman, Craig Copeland, and Jack VanDerhei, "The 2011 Retirement Confidence Survey: Confidence Drops to Record Lows, Reflecting 'the New Normal,'" EBRI Issue Brief no. 355, March 2011.
2. "Dementia Risk Reduced by Putting Off Retirement, Study Suggests," July 15, 2013. Copyright © 2013 CBS Interactive Inc. All rights reserved. www.cbsnews.com/8301-204_162-57593751/dementia-risk-reduced-by-putting-off-retirement-study-suggests/.

Chapter 8

1. Leisa D. Sargent, Mary Dean Lee, Bill Martin, and Jelena Zikic, "Reinventing Retirement: New Pathways, New Arrangements, New Meanings." *Human Relations* 66, no. 1 (2013): 3–21. http://hum.sagepub.com/content/66/1/3.abstract?patientinform-links=yes&legid=sphum;66/1/3.
2. Ron Zemke, Claire Raines, and Bob Filipczak, *Generations at Work: Managing the Clash of Veterans, Boomers, Xers, and Nexters in Your Workplace,* 2nd ed. (New York: AMACOM, 2013).
3. Linda Gravett and Robin Throckmorton, *Bridging the Generation Gap: How to Get Radio Babies, Boomers, Gen Xers, and Gen Yers to Work Together and Achieve More* (Pompton Plains, NJ: Career Press, 2007).
4. Kevin Kinsella and Victoria A. Velkoff, *An Aging World: 2001.* U.S. Census Bureau, Series P95/01-1 (Washington, DC: U.S. Government Printing Office, 2001).
5. David Bloom and David Canning, "How Companies Must Adapt for an Aging Workforce." *Harvard Business Review,* December 3, 2012. http://blogs.hbr.org/cs/2012/12/how_companies_must_adapt_for_a.html.
6. Diane Erickson, "Learning in Retirement Peer Instructors: In Over Their Heads or Swimming Comfortably?" *Educational Gerontology* 35 (2009): 393–408. Copyright © Taylor & Francis Group, LLC. ISSN: 0360-1277 print=1521-0472 online, http://www.tandfonline.com/toc/uedg20/current.
7. "The Cracked Nest Egg: The Retirement Outlook of the Unemployed & Underemployed," *13th Annual Transamerica Retirement Survey.* Copyright © Transamerica Center for Retirement Studies, 2012. www.transamericacenter.org/resources/The%20Cracked%20Nest%20Egg%20_%20FINAL_July%2018%202012.pdf.
8. Richard W. Johnson, Janette Kawachi, and Eric K. Lewis, "Older Workers on the Move: Recareering in Later Life." Copyright © 2009, AARP. www.urban.org/uploadedpdf/1001272_olderworksonthmove.pdf.

9. Rebecca Perron, "Staying Ahead of the Curve 2013: AARP Multicultural Work and Career Study," February 2013, AARP. www.aarp.org/work/on-the-job/info-01-2013/staying-ahead-curve-work.html.
10. Kauffman Index of Entrepreneurial Activity, www.kauffman.org/research-and-policy/kauffman-index-of-entrepreneurial-activity.aspx.
11. Andrea Coombes, "10 Tips for Boomers to Become Entrepreneurs," *Marketwatch*, January 14, 2013. www.marketwatch.com/story/10-tips-for-boomers-to-become-entrepreneurs-2013-01-14.
12. Ibid.
13. Ibid.

Chapter 9

1. Max Chafkin, "True to Its Roots: Why Kickstarter Won't Sell," *Fast Company*, April 2013. www.fastcompany.com/3006694/where-are-they-now/true-to-its-roots-why-kickstarter-wont-sell.
2. John Wallis Rowe and Robert L. Kahn, *Successful Aging* (New York: Dell, 1999).

Chapter 10

1. Leisa D. Sargent, Mary Dean Lee, Bill Martin, and Jelena Zikic, "Reinventing Retirement: New Pathways, New Arrangements, New Meanings," *Human Relations* 66, no. 1 (2013): 13. http://hum.sagepub.com/content/vol66/issue1/?etoc
2. www.statisticbrain.com/gym-membership-statistics/.
3. Michael B. Frisch, *Quality of Life Therapy: Applying a Life Satisfaction Approach to Positive Psychology and Cognitive Therapy* (Hoboken, NJ: John Wiley & Sons, 2005).

Chapter 11

1. Robert Frank, "What's Rich? Depends on How Old (and Rich) You Are," January 29, 2013. www.cnbc.com/id/100415923.
2. "U.S. Trust 2013 Insights on Wealth and Worth," www.ustrust.com/ust/Pages/Insights-on-Wealth-and-Worth-2013.aspx.

Chapter 14

1. Christopher T. Robertson, Richard Egelhof, and Michael Hoke, "Get Sick, Get Out: The Medical Causes of Home Foreclosures." *Health Matrix* 18 (2008): 65–105. Available at http://works.bepress.com/christopher_robertson/2.

Chapter 16

1. Dalbar Inc., "2013 QAIB," April 2013.
2. Jason W. Douthit, "Participant Directed Accounts versus Trustee Directed Accounts: Why Employers Should Consider Trustee Directed 401(k) Plans," *Pension Trends Newsletter*, February 2013. www.independentactuaries.com/resources/pension-trends-newsletter/.
3. "Class Act," April 1, 2000. www.thinkadvisor.com/2000/04/01/class-act.

Chapter 17

1. Dr. Michael F. Roizen, *Real Age* (New York: HarperCollins, 1999).
2. John Wallis Rowe and Robert L. Kahn, *Successful Aging* (New York: Dell, 1999).
3. The Regents of the University of Michigan, "Health and Retirement Study." http://hrsonline.isr.umich.edu/index.php?p=dbook.
4. Roger A. Fielding, W. Jack Rejeski, Steven Blair, et al. for the LIFE Research Group, "The Lifestyle Interventions and Independence for Elders Study: Design and Methods," *Journal of Gerontology* 66A (November 2011): 1226–37.
5. B. M. Brown, J. J. Peiffer, H. R. Sohrabi, et al., "Intense Physical Activity Is Associated with Cognitive Performance in the Elderly," *Translational Psychiatry* 2 (2012): e191, doi:10.1038/tp.2012.118. www.nature.com/tp/journal/v2/n11/pdf/tp2012118a.pdf.
6. Phyllis Moen, William A. Erickson, Madhurima Agarwal, Vivian Fields, and Laurie Todd, *The Cornell Retirement and Well-Being Study: Final Report* (Ithaca, NY: Bronfenbrenner Life Course Center, Cornell University, 2000). http://worlddatabaseofhappiness.eur.nl/hap_bib/freetexts/moen_p_2000.pdf.

About the Author

Mitch Anthony is the founder and president of mitchanthony.com, an organization dedicated to showing companies how to communicate openly and honestly with their clients and customers.

For more than a decade, Mitch has shown individuals how to move from a financial plan focused strictly on the numbers (return on assets) to one focused on Return on Life™ (ROL)—living the life you want with the money you have. He personally consults with many of the largest and most recognized names in the financial services industry on ROL planning and relationship development.

Mitch has been named one of the financial services industry's top "Movers & Shakers" for his pioneering work regarding financial life planning. He has partnered with numerous universities in the United States and Canada to develop financial life planning programs for their undergraduate programs. Mitch is a popular speaker and contributor to both local and national media and host of the inspirational radio feature *The Daily Dose,* heard on approximately 100 radio stations nationwide.

A prolific author, Mitch has written more than 10 books. *The Cash in the Hat* (Insights Press) has been adopted for use in a program that teaches children about the importance of financial responsibility.

Mitch and his wife, Debbie, live in Rochester, Minnesota, where they are involved in many philanthropic endeavors at both the local and international level. Living examples of the new retirementality, neither Mitch nor Debbie has plans to ever retire.

For more information about Mitch and his organization, visit www.mitchanthony.com, or contact him at Mitch@mitchanthony.com.

Index